Live, Laugh, Lesbian

of related interest

Gay Man Talking
All the Conversations We Never Had
Daniel Harding
ISBN 978 1 83997 094 8
eISBN 978 1 83997 095 5

I Am Ace
Advice on Living Your Best Asexual Life
Cody Daigle-Orians
ISBN 978 1 83997 262 1
eISBN 978 1 83997 263 8

Bisexual Men Exist
A Handbook for Bisexual, Pansexual and M-Spec Men
Vaneet Mehta
ISBN 978 1 78775 719 6
eISBN 978 1 78775 720 2

How to Understand Your Sexuality
A Practical Guide for Exploring Who You Are
Meg-John Barker and Alex Iantaffi
ISBN 978 1 78775 618 2
eISBN 978 1 78775 619 9

Live, Laugh, Lesbian

Navigating Life as a Lesbian in the 21st Century

Helen Scott

Jessica Kingsley Publishers
London and Philadelphia

First published in Great Britain in 2024 by Jessica Kingsley Publishers
An imprint of John Murray Press

1

Copyright © Helen Scott 2024

A CIP catalogue record for this title is available from the British
Library and the Library of Congress

ISBN 978 1 83997 814 2
eISBN 978 1 83997 815 9

Printed and bound in Great Britain by Clays Ltd

Jessica Kingsley Publishers' policy is to use papers that are natural,
renewable and recyclable products and made from wood grown
in sustainable forests. The logging and manufacturing processes
are expected to conform to the environmental regulations
of the country of origin.

Jessica Kingsley Publishers
Carmelite House
50 Victoria Embankment
London EC4Y 0DZ

www.jkp.com

John Murray Press
Part of Hodder & Stoughton Limited
An Hachette UK Company

To my LGBTQ+ family: this book is for you. To know that you are loved, worthy and extraordinarily beautiful, just as you are.

And to the Famalam, my online family, my daily inspiration. Thank you for being with me every step of the way.

Contents

Preface

Throughout the course of this book you'll find that I've called upon some of my favourite queer humans from around the world to share some of their personal stories with us. I won't lie, I had a few fangirl moments interviewing these awesome people, but I digress. These inserts were important firstly because as a white, blonde, femme presenting woman, not to diminish my own experiences, there are some struggles that you might face that I won't have. And it's important to me that you feel seen, that you can relate to more than just our shared queerness, and so I hope in adding in these precious personal accounts from others that it showcases not only diversity in our journeys and experiences, but ultimately a consistent outcome of feeling happy in who you are and living authentically in your own skin. And that is exactly what the contributors to this book feel. They may have had ups and downs, personal struggles and things to overcome, but ultimately all of us feel grateful to be exactly who we are. I know I can speak for everyone who so kindly added to this book that you can overcome anything, and that your pursuit for self-acceptance and self-love is the most beautiful gift that you can give to yourself.

Chapter 1

When I was nine, I had a best friend who, for the purposes of this story, we'll call Flower. Flower was bold and intelligent, with really shiny, straight auburn hair. She laughed hard at my slapstick-style humour and stuck up for me when the boys teased us in the playground. We'd have sleepovers, eat sweets, play dress up, and watch cartoons like all the other kids in my school. But what we also did, which I didn't do with my other school friends, was kiss each other. A lot.

We'd go to her house after school and act out these Disney-esque scenes, me saving her from dragons, her fighting off an army of trolls. We'd battle wizards, play fairy godmothers and always end by waking each other with a kiss. The kiss would turn into more kissing, and it soon became our favourite part of the game, obvs.

Now you might instantly be transported back to your own childhood here. Maybe not to your own secret snogging story like mine, but flutterings. A friend you *really* liked playing with, or becoming obsessed with your favourite female TV or film character (cough, Missy from *Bring It On*). This is where a lot of our stories begin, if you're a lesbian like me or if you sit anywhere on the queer spectrum; this is often how it starts. Naive, innocent kids, navigating childhood amongst the first throngs of social norms that were being thrown at us. Navigating the rights and wrongs we were taught. I know that for a lot of us we knew very quickly that something about how we felt was 'different', and yet, here you are reading this book today. So a little gay hooray for even turning the first page!

The first time I kissed Flower, we started with our hands over our mouths and just kind of bumped our palms together. That then progressed to lip-on-lip contact, which felt dangerous, and exciting, and was just about as far as we dared to go. I mean, at the age of nine, kissing is no passionate embrace, let's be real. It was just curiosity at this point. Two innocent baby souls, exploring something that we knew even then wasn't considered 'normal'. Besides the fact that Flower was a girl, kissing in general seemed kind of naughty at that age. It was something adults did in movies, or that your parents did occasionally whilst you and your siblings made noises pretending to be sick. Even aged nine, I knew physical contact in that way had a few different meanings, but it most certainly wasn't 'normal' for me to be snogging Flower after school in matching Cinderella outfits in a fort made out of bed sheets. And so it all stayed inside my wee little heart, and we never acknowledged it outside of those games we played together.

For a lot of us, looking back on our childhoods, we probably can't remember the *precise* moment we realized fancying the same sex was considered wrong. It was just something that *was*. Whether it was boys calling girls lesbians in the playground or feeling a rush of heat to my face when holding a girl's hand and hoping no one would notice. Thankfully for me, there wasn't any homophobia being thrown around at home, but I still knew that it wasn't right for two girls to kiss. And isn't it crazy to know that social conditioning can infiltrate a little person's brain so easily and unconsciously? When you're that age, and feeling those feelings, there's not much else that could make a child feel so isolated. But of course, now, I know that I *wasn't* alone.

This book is not an autobiography, but it *is* anecdotal. It's important for me to share my stories with you, first so that you can start to realize just how similar we all are; even when our journeys are different, we are all connected by this beautiful uniqueness that we've been born with. But second because I've been a right messy cow over the years and have some hilarious stories to share with you that I know you'll love! No, but really, hearing my story, I hope, is going to ease your soul, show you that we are all in the same boat – the minority, yes, but the community! Your LGBTQ+ family. It's my mission for you to know that, by the end of this book, no matter what, you are loved. Your sexuality doesn't have to be something that causes you continual pain or defines your entire life and experiences. I can't deny that it will impact your life, but the default isn't, and shouldn't be, that it does so negatively.

Growing up in the nineties (yes, I know, a long, long time ago) was completely binary, which is one of the reasons why I knew that what I was doing wasn't considered normal. Boys wore blue and girls wore pink; boys were strong and girls were pretty; Barbie kissed Ken and the princess always fell in love with the prince. And so it was very clear, even as a child, that it was out of the ordinary for two girls to be doing what Flower and I were doing.

Now let's face it: the world today is still hugely binary at large, but back when I was at school, me and all my peers had parents who were born in the fifties and sixties and lived through times when it was still illegal to be gay, same-sex marriage hadn't been introduced and most people thought HIV was a 'gay man's disease'*. And so that systemic history of what a man and a woman should be was hugely prevalent in my childhood, because all of my peers were learning lessons from parents who had homophobia ingrained into them, knowingly or not. So even at the age of nine, when I didn't know much of the world, when my experiences were limited to what I was exposed to at school, on the television and from what my parents taught me, 'lesbian' was not something I wanted to be.

One breaktime at school, a boy tried to hold Flower's hand in the playground, and I kneed him in the balls. I think that may have been one of my first pangs of romantic jealousy! I simply saw it as me being a close and loyal friend, the kind of girl-gang vibe only Taylor Swift and her posse know about, the kind of friend who would stick up for you no matter what. Of course now I know that I was just, in fact, a raging lesbian. A baby gay, having my first experience of kissing and crushing on other girls and feeling the feels. I had no way of understanding what it all meant. I had no one I felt I could talk to about it, no TV shows or magazines to watch or look at that reflected similar behaviours to my own. And although it was a secret, deep down I didn't feel like what I was doing was *wrong*; in fact, it felt extremely 'normal', which was super confusing and only deepened that feeling of 'other' inside me. It starts to teach you that you're different for feeling the way that you feel, to try to control the way you're perceived

---

* HIV is a virus, not a disease.

by others for fear of being found out, and ultimately to start hiding parts of yourself. It actually taught me to be extremely secretive, and to almost compartmentalize my life to an extent. 'I can be this person with these people, and I can be this person with Flower, and I can be this person to my parents.' I mean, children shouldn't be having to think about these things. Although, as a 'look for the positives' kinda gal, it made me the friend who you can go to about anything and I won't judge you, which led me to being your lesbian big sister, and to writing this book. So even if baby Helen suffered in those early years, I really think it all happened in that way for a reason.

Now I have to confess that as well as Flower, I was also kissing boys. I know, how could I? But let me explain. My boy crushes were on androgynous, feminine-energy boys, which totally makes sense as that's my type now, but in women. My point is, because of those feelings, those fancies and those experiences with boys, I didn't realize that I was a *lesbian*. I didn't even think I was bisexual; I just had absolutely no idea. For me this wasn't a denial phase, which I know some of us experience, and understandably so, but I think it was more of a naivety phase. I now realize that I didn't know I was a lesbian because I didn't really *know* what a lesbian was. I had boyfriends, one of whom I stalked around my secondary school for four months every lunchtime, following him to the art department and feigning a love of anime so that he would notice me. He was very Harry Styles energy in my defence! But even up until the age of seventeen I had boyfriends, fancied Nick from Backstreet Boys and just didn't know that I was, in fact, gayer than a Fletcher concert.

Everybody's experience of understanding their sexuality is different. Some people are born knowing that they only like girls, some develop crushes and realize in their school years and some people make it through half of their lives before realizing much further down the line. There is no 'right time' to have a eureka moment about your sexuality, and, as we'll discuss later, sexuality is far more fluid and changeable than you think, so it might just hit you one day when you aren't looking. Just as all humans look different, just as we all butter our toast slightly differently, we all *feel* things differently, too. We all have our own beautiful journeys with our sexuality, and what is important to know is that whatever your way is, that's the right way for you. Your journey is utterly unique, utterly personal and utterly perfect, my love.

When I started secondary school, I bid Flower farewell, and it was a few years before I had my next girl-on-girl moment with my new best friend, kissing her at a sleepover. It only happened one time, and the same 'hand covering mouth action' occurred, but the difference of course was that now, I was at senior school. I was a little older, a little wiser and a little more scared of not fitting in. As we all know, senior school is bloody hard. I remember doing anything and everything I could to get through it without sticking out too much, and I know that's how most of us felt. Being a teenager is one of the hardest things you go through in life, and so I obvs didn't want a soul to find out about me and my bezza having our late-night lipsing session. Whilst we may have similar experiences, we all travel on our own unique paths to Gay Town, and so even when my pattern of behaviour continued into senior school, the word lesbian didn't crop up once in the way that I viewed myself. It wasn't a term that ever crossed my mind when I was having these cheeky snogs, which probably sounds mental, 'cause, duh?! But honestly, any connotation of what a lesbian 'looked like' back then just didn't match with who I was, and this is where representation is just so important.

Lesbians in my youth were portrayed as butch, short-haired, lumberjack-shirt-wearing older women. Which, funnily enough, is right up my alley these days. I was a very feminine-presenting teen, totally in touch with my femininity, I loved fashion and make up and all things that were considered 'girly', and so my mind simply never registered an association. We didn't have social media twenty years ago where we could find a variety of lesbians (and their cats) on any continent or in any city or rural town in the world. Add to that, I had never even *met* any lesbians irl in my teens. Lesbians were kind of fictional in a way, something boys called you in the playground, or sexualized on Pornhub; lesbians were kind of like the Tooth Fairy. A myth.

The fact that I'd never met a lesbian irl was so integral to me not realizing my sexuality because something that I've learned about my sexuality over the years is that I'm only attracted to lesbians/queer people. Not in a fetishized sense, but in a 'Why would I fancy a straight woman?' kind of way. This is a really intricate part of my sexuality that may differ to yours, but I'll say it again and again: sexuality is not a one-size-fits-all, and whatever you feel is perfectly normal for you. I actually made a TikTok about it and found a whole tribe of lesbians who feel the same way, but in the same breath there's a whole community of lesbians who are bang into straight women. Each to their own! And so back then I didn't process my kissing other girls as me being lesbian or even bisexual; I just thought it was probably something everyone else had done or was doing and was just a bit of fun.

My life was about to be turned upside down when I met my first actual lesbian...

By the time I was fifteen I was part of a girl gang: a group of totally straight, Friday night clubbing, boy-mad gals, and I slotted right in! I'd started to wear heels and push-up bras and was very much influenced by my love for *Sex and the City*. Not very 'gay' by stereotypical standards. *But*, alongside my gal pals, I'd also become friends with Emy and Rob, my co-stars in the school drama club who were both camp as chips and super fun to be around. Rob was a gay boy through and through, not yet out, but his love for the *Little Mermaid* mixed with a red lip told you everything you needed to know. Emy, on the other hand, was a year older than us and was popular. But not just popular. Popular, and *gay*. It was like some sort of early 2000s miracle.

Thankfully things now are very different to when I was at school, in large part due to all of the work our previous generations have put into protesting for our rights and more recently the activity and community building on TikTok. And nowadays over 21 per cent of American Gen Zs consider themselves part of the LGBTQ+ spectrum, and in England and Wales, Gen Z are twice as likely to identify as LGBTQ+ than they were in the previous Census, according to the 2023 Census. They're utterly incredible figures! Regardless of what age you are reading this, I think we can all feel the cultural shift from the past decade in how we are perceived and portrayed, even though there is always much further to go. But back to 2005...

I was fifteen and had finally met a lesbian, for real, in the flesh! And look, I don't want to play into the stereotype that all lesbians end up hooking up, but I fancied her! She was so out, so confident, so talented and honestly, at first I didn't realize I was crushing. But the more I got to know her and spent time with her, the more I started to act weird in her presence. You know what I'm talking about, right? I found myself scanning the playground and hallways constantly so that I could go up to and speak to her. I started to not know what to say around her; she made me nervous and I wanted to impress her all the time. Slowly I started to understand that I was falling in love with her. A girl!

It was only Rob who knew I was crushing hard on our friend. I'd felt confident enough to confide in him but otherwise had no idea what to do about it. The fear of the social impact it would have on my life if anybody found out drove me to keep my feelings locked up tight in my heart. I didn't necessarily think there would be truly horrific repercussions if anybody found out, but the 'not knowing' was enough for me to keep it to myself. There was also a part of me that needed the time and space to figure out these feelings in my own head, by myself, before sharing them with others. Until one summer evening, on a night out with the three of us, I suddenly felt brave. I was getting the tingles, the vagina tingles. I knew it was finally time to say something, and so, overcome with the urge that had been building up inside of me for weeks, stood outside the takeaway shop, I kissed her. Romantic, right?

That night sparked a love affair that lasted three whole glorious months. My once-innocent girl-on-girl experiences were now blown out of the water by my first proper lesbian snog, which led to the first time I ever touched a vagina other than my own. Zero to one hundred, real fast! More on that in Chapter 4, but what I will say is, wow. Why are women's mouths so great?! My three-month secret lesbian love affair was a whirlwind of emotions, and as you can imagine it was the most exciting, terrifying and elating thing that had ever happened to me. We would send letters to one another, she wrote me poetry, we brushed hands in the corridors and stole kisses behind the curtains of the drama studio. It was a real queer teenage romance. Netflix, get at me! And all the while I was living my very straight life, with my very straight friends, dreading the idea of anyone finding out what I was really up to at the weekends.

First love bangs hard, period, but for baby gays I'm afraid it's even tougher. We're battling a whole mixture of emotions on top of what should be a beautiful feeling. You may feel (or have felt) ashamed, embarrassed or angry, which makes me ache for all of us. It should be one of the most glorious experiences of our lives, and yet, to go through all of those intricacies as well as falling hard can tarnish things. Luckily for the all the bay gays to come, society feels like it's heading more and more in the right direction, but it can be said unanimously around the globe, regardless of gender or sexuality: you never forget your first love.

Meet Emily...

I'm Emily Gracin, my pronouns are she/they and the labels I use are either queer or lesbian.

I was with someone who was still in the closet when I first dated women. I felt this constant push and pull between wanting to respect her choices and her situation and wanting to respect my own need to be seen for who I truly am. It was hard because we both loved each other but had completely different needs when it came to expressing our own identities. I ended up coming out individually, even whilst we were still dating, and whilst that felt amazing, it was upsetting because I was unable to share that experience with my partner. I wanted to be able to tell the world how much I loved her and show her off just how any other couple would, so it hurt to be out of the closet with one hand still reaching in the closet for my partner. However, it taught me a lot about sacrifice and putting those you love before you, circumstantially. I think at the end of the day, there is no right or wrong in this situation, it's personal choice.

When I first came out as a lesbian, I had this idea that I needed to dress and act ultra-masculine. I went through a 'hey mamas' phase, as the internet likes to call it. I started dressing in ways that I actually didn't fully identify with but felt I had to in order to validate my sexuality. My personality even changed, too. I remember becoming extremely uncomfortable being vulnerable with my naturally feminine personality; I put up this 'tough guy' persona that was never truly me. With time I've learned that in reality, no persona, no clothes and no attitude validates your sexuality. If you're gay, you're just simply gay!

These days I dress pretty androgynous and that's where I feel the most comfortable. I get a lot of compliments on how I am able to dress masc whilst keeping my very feminine personality, and I will say that did take some time. It's hard when society tries to push everyone into a binary, but staying true to yourself is what will always leave you feeling most comfortable.

In recent years, the only new friends I take on are queer. It's not specifically on purpose, but once you make one gay friend, you make another, and another, and before you know it, you know *all* the lesbians in LA (I live in Los Angeles, CA). Genuinely, it's really, really great. As much as I love to make fun of straight people in my comedy, I have nothing against them; I simply just cannot relate. Having close friends who understand the intricate dynamics of women loving women (wlw) relationships is so helpful, not to mention validating. Especially when you are struggling with relationship issues, hetero relationships are simply so different from homo ones, and having homo friends who understand that makes all the difference.

I mostly identify with the word lesbian, but sometimes I don't! The truth is me being disinterested in men has nothing to do with physicality. I always say I feel like I have the capacity to be pansexual but I just have to work through my visceral disgust for men (who they are as people, on the inside). But who is to say I won't meet a man one day (with a feminine, woman-like personality) and fall head over heels for him? Okay, I very much doubt it but, never say never! The point is, I don't love using labels because things can change over time. I am not opposed to dating gender nonconforming people either, so technically that also wouldn't make me a true 'lesbian'. I honestly just say whatever rolls off the tongue easiest to broadcast, for example, 'HEY, I LIKE WOMEN.'

I have to say I am lucky enough to live in a place like LA, which is very liberal and 'with the times'. I don't face too much stigma here when it comes to my sexuality. The only stigma I face from time to time comes with dating. Sometimes when I go on a date with a more femme woman, since I present more masculine, they expect me to act like a man and can treat me as one, too. They want me to pay for every meal, they don't care to satisfy me in bed, etc. Just because I present more masculine doesn't mean I'm not a woman too!

Sexuality is a spectrum and is ever changing. It's okay to explore new avenues of your identity, whether it's your gender expression or your sexuality. God is a real homie for making me gay. Shout out to him; he's a cool dude.

Emma Gracin

Nowadays I'm immersed in LGBTQ+ culture, lifestyle and community, and speaking candidly about my own experiences has led me to realize that secret affairs are often a lot of people's first explorations of sexuality. High five if you're a secret affair twin! No, but really, having to hide something so pure and natural has its impact on us as we grow into adulthood, and I've done a lot of reflection over the years. Something that has helped me evolve into the confident, out and proud lesbian I am today is giving love to baby Helen. Sounds woo woo, but I'm going to talk you through how to do the same thing, step by step, before the end of this book, because honestly, it's life changing. Looking back and showering yourself with acceptance, understanding and, if necessary, forgiveness, is incredibly good for your soul because those first navigations into becoming who you are are often the hardest.

As we've discussed, our formative years have a true and lasting impact on who we become in adulthood; however, I don't think that the beliefs we have, or that have been thrust upon us by the outside world, need to live in our hearts forever. I was scared to be myself at fifteen; I was too scared to come out to my friends and peers and say, 'This is how I feel and this is what I'm doing.' I was very much in the closet and afraid to be associated with the word lesbian and yet, here I am today, actively dismantling homophobia and sexism in a world that dared me not to even try. Hooray! And just because you start out as one thing doesn't mean you can't change and grow. Just look at the style evolution of Miley Cyrus! No, but seriously, looking back, the emotions I was experiencing when I'd met Emy and my mind was being blown by the idea that I fancied her made it feel like there would be only negative consequences. My social status could be impacted, my relationships with friends and family could be impacted and I could be shunned in my final years of my school life. It was a terrifying thing. If only I had known that what I was experiencing was perfectly normal – was beautiful even – and that thousands of other young people were going through a similar experience to me, too. What a difference that could have made to my life. It might not have changed the course of actions I took, but knowing that more people felt like me, knowing that 'lesbian' wasn't a negative word and seeing more people living their lives happily and openly may have led me to feel less ashamed or guilty.

I don't begrudge my journey; I don't look back with regret. But what is important to me now is encouraging people like you to love who you are and to be yourself so that you can live the fullest life possible without those negative feelings that I had or hiding yourself like I did. I will say this over and over again throughout this book until it's part of your everyday language, as it's something not enough people realize: life is short. Three simple words, but you have to take them seriously. You don't realize just how short it is when you're young; I only began to realize just how short life is at the age of thirty-two. But I'm telling you, it flies by! Even if you're in your thirties too, or beyond, you could do with reminding sometimes, I'm sure. And I don't say this to scare you, but I want it to light a fire under your ass to encourage you to be happy, today. Now. As soon as you possibly can be. You are who you are, you were born exactly how you were meant to be and having a different sexuality to the majority of your peers is completely and utterly normal. In fact, it's a blessing. When your sexuality is a secret, when you only have your own thoughts in your own head to converse with, it can feel like you're the only gay in the world, let alone in the village. And I'm here to tell you that you're not. You are one of thousands, hundreds of thousands, of beautiful queer humans, and whether you want to tell those in your reality or you want to find your online community to chat to, we're here and ready to listen. You most definitely are not alone.

Looking back on our childhoods is just the first part of our journey to freeing ourselves of any negative feelings that we might experience about who we are, and in all of the chapters to come, I'm giving you some actionable steps to being able to reach your most fulfilled self. To finish this first chapter I want you to look back on 'baby you', and in the most loving and caring way, think about all that they've gotten you through. I want you to focus on the magic and to write a letter to yourself on the blank page after this one. I want you to focus on all of those incredible interactions and feelings and memories you've shared – your first crush, your first love, stolen kisses or your coming-out story if you have one – and to write to them telling them how proud you are of how they've handled themselves. How proud you are of them for getting you to where you are today. And to promise them you're going to do everything in your power to live the happiest and most fulfilled life possible, because they deserve it. Write with the intention that one day, this book could end up in a thrift store, or on a bookshelf in a coffee shop, and this is your very own addition to *Live, Laugh, Lesbian* that could be just what a baby gay who happens to pick it up needs to hear. Letter writing can trigger powerful emotions, so set up a calm and relaxing space to do it in and do your best to be as honest as you possibly can. You deserve to love who you are, to accept who you are and to know that you might never have all the answers, you might never have the acceptance from everyone you seek, but if you truly love yourself, you will always have *you* to rely on. And that is a beautiful thing.

I look back on baby Helen and I'm so proud of her. She had no freaking clue what was going on; she just wanted to make people laugh, to have fierce and wild friendships, and to be loved for who she was. I've had a lot of questions looking back on my early years. Why didn't I identify my sexuality earlier? Why didn't I talk to my parents about it? Why didn't I feel brave enough to tell my peers about my true feelings? And I've given myself time and space to work through the answers to those questions so that I can better understand myself and love who I am with a deeper respect than ever. So I want to encourage you, no matter how painful or inconsequential you feel it may be, to do it. Look back on your younger self and give them some damn credit for making it this far. My wish is for you to get to the end of this book, and think, bloody hell, I love being me! So wherever you're at with your sexuality, you picked up a book with the word lesbian in the title, and honestly, I just know baby you would be so proud.

Dear baby ....

....

....

....

....

....

....

....

....

....

....

....

....

....

....

....

....

....

....

....

....

Chapter 2

Coming Out and Embracing You

Terrifying. That's one word I've heard a lot when talking to my queer peers about coming out, and terrifying it can definitely be. The idea of baring your soul, your deepest self, and laying it out on a table for people to judge you? Terrifying, I get it. However, what if, rather than thinking about it as something to be 'found out', you think about it as gifting people with a piece of information and showing them a beautiful part of yourself? That actually, you're bestowing them with a magical and gorgeous piece of knowledge about you that they should be privileged to hold. Would it feel so terrifying then? Coming out, in the beginning, might just be being looked at with the wrong perspective.

I know, I'm sounding a bit woo woo over here, and like, 'Oh yeah! That would be a lovely way to think about things in fantasy land, but please rejoin us here in the real world, Helen, where it feels like sticks and stones can, and absolutely will, break my bones.' I get it, promise. But ultimately, the journey we're on together throughout this book is to come to a place where you love yourself so hard that what people think and feel about you is so secondary that you can join me in this very real place called 'Eff you if you don't like it'!

Let's jump back to spring 2007. I was seventeen and hurtling towards the end of my first year at dance college. Think of the series *Glee*, or, if you're too young for that, just a whole lot of jazz hands and singing loudly at every opportunity, and it was basically that but with far more broken toes and sweaty dance thongs. I had broken up with my boyfriend, a tall and androgynous gentle soul, a bass player and my first real stab at a relationship. He was sweet and lovely, but to be frank, he never made me come. And so, without connecting any dots, I let him go and as the summer holidays began, I got a part-time job at a local pub. And this is where my coming-out story begins.

Day one on the job and I'd never been a waitress before. I was great with customers but, honestly, crap with the actual tasks. I put things through the till wrong, I wasn't on top of timings and I was a spiller. So yeah, I wasn't great, but I was getting a kick out of earning some money, prancing around and chatting away with the customers. Anyway, I go to the bar to pick up some drinks, and that's when I saw her. Short, dark hair; cute, nerdy glasses; a neckerchief (forgive her, it was 2007, after all); and a lip stud. My bar manager, Jess. The fittest thing I'd ever seen in my life.

I was instantly besotted. Like, a bit scarily so in the way only lesbians know how to be. I'd never fancied someone so intensely in my entire life. Even Emy, my schooltime affair, hadn't given me the vagina tingles I got when I saw Jess. From that moment on I couldn't get her out of my brain; I thought about her at home, in the shower, while doing my laundry. In particular, I needed to know what kissing her felt like. The one problem I had was that she couldn't stand me. No, really, she hated me. Whilst my co-workers were patient with my apparent lack of waitressing skills, Jess was the opposite and didn't hold back in sharing how annoying she found me.

As the weeks went by, my friendship with my floor manager, Martin, strengthened and I learned that he and Jess were best friends and lived together in the flat above the pub. I was desperate to spend some time with her out of work to let her see the bedazzling and hilarious me, and by this point I had begun flirting with her as best you can with someone who will barely look at you, let alone acknowledge your existence.

Now, let's pause for thought here. Until this point, I was 'straight' in my eyes. I was seventeen, had had boyfriends and was convinced I was into androgynous, Kurt Cobain types with long hair and wistful vibes. The romance from my schooltime affair with Emy seemed a lifetime ago, and I'd convinced myself up to this point that it was a one-time thing, a teenage experiment. And yet, here I was absolutely dying for my female bar manager, four years my senior. What on earth was happening?

Looking back, I still get goosebumps thinking about it. In the space of a few weeks, my identity had been completely dismantled and yet I felt like the entire world had aligned around me. It was like finally seeing the answer to a really long maths equation or waking up from a very intense dream and focusing back on reality. I know that sounds dramatic, but my whole world finally made sense, even though I'd never realized that it hadn't before. If you're someone who hasn't realized your sexuality until later in life, whether you've come out or not, then you understand. When you finally realize it, or acknowledge it, it's like seeing things in colour rather than in black and white.

It's not always glaringly obvious that you're gay, and because of stigma and homophobia and the potential ramifications that can ensue, it's not a conclusion you land upon lightly. A lot of people, when they come out, have friends and family say, 'Oh, we always knew!' and the person themself can't understand how. It's not always easy to see something from the inside out – it's like being better at offering advice than taking your own – and mix that with a splash of denial and you might end up with a lightbulb moment like mine. But thankfully, and importantly, there's absolutely no correct timeline for discovering, accepting or acknowledging your sexuality. The journey you have with your sexuality has no timeframe, time limit or right or wrong. It's simply your journey.

One evening, Martin invited me on a night out with some of my colleagues to the local gay bar that, unbeknownst to me, was five minutes away from where I had lived my entire life. Who knew? I don't know if it was because it was summer, I was feeling young and reckless or if I was just so ready to dive headfirst into my newfound female-focused feelings, but I had this overwhelming confidence and decided that I was going to kiss Jess that night. I was a woman with a mission. A lesbian James Bond, if you will.

I was in a unique position, feeling excited by newfound sexuality. I am so aware of that. Hearing my peers' very different and, oftentimes traumatic, coming-out experiences are in part what has led me to write this book. It's what has spurred me on over the years to be the big sister you need to go to for advice, to champion queerness and be an out and proud ambassador for the community. I know I am so very lucky to walk in my shoes, and as much as I'm grateful to be able to tell you this story of acceptance, I am able to feel your pain and am here to help pick you up and cherish you if your story doesn't align with my own.

I turned up, ready for the night out, my first ever venture to a gay bar, excited and nervous but with one thing burning on my mind. Jess was less than impressed to see that I was joining them, but little did she know about my plan to not only change how she saw me but to fulfil what I'd been thinking about for so long... What that mouth do? Oh, to be young and have that feeling of invincibility! It was my make-or-break moment. And Famalam, thank the vagina gods for my bravery, because Jess and I *did* kiss that night, and, despite her initial loathing of me, a two-year relationship ensued with all of my lesbian firsts being experienced in one of the most beautiful relationships of my life.

It was a whirlwind era, and I can't quite remember the nitty-gritty details, the in-between bit of turning Jess's hatred into love, and so I asked her because of course as true lesbians, we're still friends.

It wasn't so much hatred, I just found you really annoying. You were always hanging around me rather than getting on with your job; I didn't realize it was because you fancied me. Then once the night out had happened, I looked at you in a different way and thought, actually, she's annoying in a good way. You were needy, you were  very persistent, that was attractive to me and you didn't give up. I also loved that you came across very sassy and feisty but

I got to see your vulnerable side. You were besotted with me so I never worried that this was your first relationship, you loved me so much.

The intensity of my first lesbian relationship can be summed up by telling you this. Jess had booked a three-month trip to Australia before she met me, and so shortly after our first kiss, off she went to the other side of the world. I was utterly lost without her, but we kept in touch via Myspace (god, I feel old) and she messaged me with updates on her travels most days. After three weeks of missing her, I was sitting in the pub one night after my shift had ended and Jess walked in! She'd cut her trip short so that we could be together, and we barely spent a day apart after that. No, you're crying! You want romance? Date a lesbian.

Meet Alissa...

My name is Alissa Butt, my pronouns are they/them and I identify as queer.

I recently changed my pronouns not too long ago, but I think I've always known that these were meant for me, I was just too scared to tell people because I didn't want to make it harder for others to understand why I changed them. I struggled for a while, always putting other people before myself in that sense, but once I let it all go and put myself first, I felt so free. I still very much consider myself a woman and love my body, but my pronouns are more based on my appearance and how I present myself, which is androgynous. I don't feel super feminine and I don't feel super masculine,

I just feel like the perfect combination of both. They/them pronouns excite me and have made me feel so comfortable with being who I am and have allowed me to be my most authentic self. Now I get to talk and share more about my journey and have that voice to be there and help others with their journey as well.

I had a great childhood and I couldn't complain, until I started to realize that I liked girls, which was probably when I was fourteen or fifteen and that's when things kinda started to get rocky with my mom.

Me and my mom butt heads a lot and we never had a super close relationship. She's an Italian woman, very strong, and she's not super emotional. Being a Cancer, I'm very sensitive and emotional. I wear my feelings and everything on my sleeve so I cry a lot. I'm a crier! So realizing that I liked girls, I started to freak out a little bit and didn't know what that meant or how to tell my family and whatnot. My mom actually caught me with a girl, that's how she found out, so I felt that probably traumatized her for a little bit.

I felt like I would have to lie to her about where I was going and who I was hanging out with. If I had friends who looked like they were gay, my mom wouldn't want me to hang out with them, It's not something I have really talked about that much because I love my mom so much and I don't want to talk badly about her. But I know it can help people in their coming out because not everyone's family is accepting.

I always felt like I was hiding so many things and lying and I hated it, but it was too hard for me to talk about with my mom because she would always get defensive and that was hard. I remember writing her letters, and she probably knew even before I did because parents aren't stupid, they know. And so I remember writing her a letter one time and it didn't go over well. And so then I went back into a shell where I just kept to myself.

Then in 2017 I was studying abroad and met someone over there, and when my family came to visit I brought her on a family trip. When I got home from that trip, I wrote my mom another letter. I was like, 'I'm gonna try this again, it needs to be a thing, she needs to know.' So I wrote her a letter, I went out to work and she texted me later that day and was just like, 'If you're happy, I'm happy.' A whole 180 out of nowhere?! And so, I don't know, maybe my family talked to her or maybe she just came to the realization herself that this was something that wasn't going to change. Maybe she thought to herself, 'I have to get over it and learn to accept it.' Who knows? However it happened, it was a 180 and it was incredible.

After that I got to bring my girlfriend over and it was just normal. It was like a light switch, and she's come such a long way since then. She's now so supportive and I can finally talk to her about girls and just be myself with her. She's now learning all of these new things (about gender) and I'm trying to teach her the best I can. I know that for a lot of parents, especially with the terms non-binary and they/them, they literally don't get it. And as much as that hurts, I just need them and my mom to respect me and then I can respect her. This is who I am.

If I could speak to baby Alissa now, I just wanna hug them so badly and just be like, 'You're okay. Everything is gonna be okay.' And, honestly, I don't know if I would say a lot besides just hug and say to them, 'People love you, you are loved and just everything is gonna be okay.'

Alissa Butt

Sometimes facing the truth of who you are is, as we've discussed, tough. Particularly if you're surrounded by homophobia, transphobia or even just a lack of understanding by those around you. You may even have, inadvertently, soaked up some internalized homophobia, taking on the negative beliefs that you were taught about the LGBTQ+ community, which can take some time to unlearn and dismantle. Settling into your identity isn't always easy and it's a sad reality that for some, coming out can mean the very worst. Being kicked out of your home, sent to conversion therapy or losing your entire family. There is often so much at stake with potentially traumatic outcomes. Being your authentic self should never come with consequences, and so it all boils down to these things: timing, patience and self-love.

Facing your sexuality does not have to be an immediate job. Deciding who you are doesn't have to be an early life decision. Taking the time to get to know yourself and to love yourself is more important than choosing a label, pressuring yourself into telling people about your sexuality and coming out to the world. Your sexuality can be private and quiet and personal, contrary to the stigma that queer people have to be loud and flamboyant all of the time. There is no timeframe when coming to terms with your sexuality, and as we'll discuss later, your sexuality may change and evolve over the course of your lifetime, but ultimately it's about listening to yourself and taking things at your own pace.

Your sexuality is about *you*. One of the biggest things you might face is worrying about what everyone else is going to think and feel, but that is secondary and even unimportant to living *your* authentic life. Remember, you didn't *choose* to be queer, and attempts to change or cover up your sexuality can be painful and sometimes damaging to your sense of self. What those around you think isn't going to change who you are on the inside; you were born with this sexuality as much as you were born with your hair and eye colour. This doesn't mean that you *have* to come out regardless of the consequences, but this part of you makes up an important aspect of your life, and if you aren't in a place where you can come out safely, it may mean some tough choices are ahead of you in order to live a full queer life.

It can feel like this ginormous part of you when you're discovering it, but you are not defined by your sexuality. Just like the rest of humankind, LGBTQ+ people have dreams, goals and ambitions. We think about what we're going to have for dinner, whether to skip leg day at the gym and how much the price of electricity has risen this year. Just as there are different skin colours throughout the human race, there are different sexualities. We don't all like the same movies, the same food, the same style of clothing. Of course we're not all going to be straight. And just because we're a minority doesn't make it wrong. Those born with an IQ of 140+ are a minority but aren't shunned by society. Those of us on this earth who are natural born athletes are a minority and not hated. It's the most natural thing to have diversity, and there is absolutely nothing wrong with you fancying someone of the same sex.

Homosexuality dates all the way back to the caveman era. Alexander the Great, according to some historians, was queer af and was king of the ancient Greek kingdom of Macedon. Oscar Wilde, gay as the day is long, was one of London's most popular playwrights in the early 1890s. Then we have lesbian royalty, Josephine Baker, a well-known entertainer of the Jazz Age. I'm telling you, we've been around since time began. Heterosexuality is just another socialized concept that has been forced upon us. Put simply, humans are animals, and much like there are gay monkeys and penguins and dolphins, we are no different.

I came to terms with my sexuality fairly quickly because my feelings for Jess were so strong I couldn't deny them. It was obvious that this is who I was because everything I felt made so much sense, what could I do but accept it? Rather than battle it, I let myself freefall into it. I'm human, so of course I wondered what people would think, and some days I felt a little self-conscious holding hands with Jess publicly, but I almost made it a point to push through those feelings because I knew in my heart that I had nothing to be ashamed of. My sexuality is a valid part of me and who I love is my own business. My happiness far outweighed the concern of who would accept me, and I've stood firmly in that since the beginning. At this point I was out to Jess and a few people at the pub, including my best friend at the time, but I hadn't actively *told* anyone yet; I hadn't officially 'come out'.

Coming out – sharing your sexuality with others – should be a choice, something to do if and when you want to. Sadly, we're not always given that option, but the steps you can take remain the same. Finding someone to talk to, a trusted friend, family member or qualified professional, is a must. As humans we crave community; we have a strong desire to feel seen by those around us, and, it may be cheesy but it's true: a problem shared is a problem halved. It can feel scary or daunting to talk about your sexuality with someone for the first time, especially if you aren't sure what they'll say or how they'll react. Take your time in choosing who that's going to be, and if you're nervous about how someone might respond, you could try asking them for their thoughts on an LGBTQ+ topic first. Talk about a particular queer celebrity or

TV show and that might help you get a feeling for whether they're likely to be supportive. You might want to consider a way to remove yourself from the conversation if you start to feel uncomfortable or overwhelmed, so thinking about *where* you're going to have this conversation might be useful, too. Even before you attempt to talk about things, write down what you'd like to say so that you can really think about what you want to share. It's also just lovely to do a little nervous brain dump!

I was quite happy with the little bubble of people who knew about my new lesbian identity for a while. I can't remember being particularly worried about telling my family, but I think I just wanted to enjoy this first sense of exploration and independence before opening up for the entire world to comment on. I stayed at the flat above the pub with Jess and one day, after many weeks and missed calls had passed, I answered the phone to my mum, who was at her wits' end. She demanded to know what was going on, why I hadn't been home, and her only conclusion was that I had gone wayward and was taking drugs or something. I was so shocked that she had been left with no other conclusion, that the words flew out of my mouth before I even had a chance to get nervous about it.

'What? Mum, no! I'm not taking drugs, I'm a lesbian!' I almost shouted it down the phone. 'I'm going out with my bar manager. Her name's Jess, she's twenty-one and she lives above the pub. That's why I've not been home!'

I heard a sigh of relief on her end before saying, 'Well, why didn't you just tell me that in the first place?'

From that moment on, Jacqueline has accepted that I'm a lesbian as much as my hair is blonde. But rather than speak for her, I thought I'd let her tell you how she felt, and what it's been like as a parent to an out and proud, loud-mouthed lesbian for the past thirty-three years:

I can clearly remember the day Helen called me to tell me that she was gay. She sounded so happy and I felt her joy! I didn't think about the homo-phobes, I naively thought everyone was the same as me – 'So what?!' I was nonplussed; love is love, in my opinion. Of course this day and age word gets around fast. Friends, col-leagues and family were mostly fine, although one colleague asked if I thought it might be a 'phase' Helen was going through, but I just laughed and said, 'Maybe?' Who cares?

I'll tell you what I've found hard: girlfriends. There isn't one that I didn't love, and there's been a few! I would say that I felt the break ups just as much as she did in some cases and really felt like her girlfriends were my girlfriends, too. You just get that female bond, I guess. Also, I don't like hearing people say to me that women shouldn't play football or rugby etc. or that they don't want to see queer actors kissing on telly. They usually apologize when I clear my throat; they (most of the time) know that my daughter is gay. They end up saying something like, 'Oh you know what I mean!' and I tell them to fuck off. Not really!

I've grown up now, boring, and am a big supporter of the LGBT community and am very proud of Helen's involvement and achievements. She's clever, beautiful, a brilliant per-former and, yes, she's gay! What more could a mother ask for?

Inherently we want to make our parents, our family, proud of us, and what's so scary is wondering or knowing that their perception of you will change. That they'll be disappointed, angry or upset and that you'll be the cause of those negative feelings, which no child wants to be. We just want to be loved and accepted and supported, and to most people, the thought of upsetting their parents is upsetting in itself. And what enhances those feelings is that your sexuality is out of your control and more often than not there's no defaulting. There's room for it to evolve and flux but ultimately it's in your DNA, and once the information is shared there's really no going back. If I were to do it again, and had my parents not been quite so open about this, there are a few ways I would have gone about it slightly differently.

Coming out to a parent, as we know, can be tough, and so I'd tell a friend or confidant first so that you have someone waiting in the wings for support and to talk about how it went afterwards. Whether you think a formal conversation or a text message or just dropping it into conversation is best, consider the avenue that makes you feel as comfortable and safe as possible. Some people decide to go full swoop and post to social media; just be prepared for lots of messages and potentially any negativity that sadly the internet can sometimes bring. But know that there are people like me out there ready to drop a bunch of rainbow emojis, too! Regardless of which way you go, it's worth considering where you'll share the news, as if that person is at work or is away on holiday, for example, they may not get back to you straight away or be able to give you the focus and energy that you'd like. Being at home gives you the privacy for everyone to be able to share their thoughts and feelings openly, whereas in public you may feel a little safer. Take the time to really think about what feels right to you.

Finding the right words can be tricky, too. You should decide if you want to be direct or casually drop it into conversation, and maybe even practise saying the words out loud until you're confident with them. You might feel a bit ridiculous looking in the mirror and telling yourself that you're a lesbian, but trust the process! You could say things like, 'I was watching a documentary about bisexual people and I really connected with some of their feelings' or 'You're important to me and I want to let you know that I'm a lesbian' or 'I've been thinking for a while and I want to let you know that I'm queer, which means I'm attracted to people of the same sex'. Saying it out loud will help you to not feel so 'cat got your tongue' in the moment, and it is also a great tool for self-assurance! Vulnerability really does induce kindness, so be honest and let them know if you feel nervous or worried, and also let them know what sort of response you're looking for. If you want to talk about it, open the conversation up for questions, or if you want some positive words of love, make it clear that that's what you need. It can really help the person you're telling to let them know where you want the conversation to go from there, a gentle nudge in the right direction.

You may need to have patience and understanding at the ready, and be prepared to have a lot of questions once you've shared your news. Someone being shocked doesn't mean that they feel unsupportive or negative towards you, but to some your news could come totally out of the blue, and everyone reacts differently when we're caught off guard. Some people just won't know what to say and that's okay; they might need some time to process. Being prepared with your boundaries is important with what you do and don't want to discuss, but being as open and forthright as you can be will certainly help.

Coming out doesn't always go well, but I want you to hold on to that self-love we're working on and try not to take any negative reactions personally. Ultimately, how someone else feels about you is because of what's going on with *them* – their own negative feelings or lack of understanding about queerness – and it doesn't have anything to do with you as a person. There may end up being different stages of acceptance from this person, and so having that friend or confidant to lean on and vent to is really important at this stage. If you feel unsafe in any way, if you're being threatened or even evicted from your home, there are a whole host of resources in the back of this book where you can seek help and guidance. No matter what situation you're in, try to connect with the community during this time. The support that is waiting for you in the arms of your LGBTQ+ siblings is so powerful and might come in extremely useful during this period.

Lastly let's go back to that thought I mentioned at the very beginning of this chapter, the sharing of your sexuality being a gift to those you love. It's a beautiful thing when you want to share something so personal and vulnerable about yourself with others, and, yes, it can be painful if that gift isn't accepted gracefully and openly, but nothing will be as painful as hiding your authentic self for the rest of your life. There is nothing more beautiful than inviting people to get to know you; it's really one of life's purposes to share your-self and to experience everything that you possibly can. And always, always remember that there's a ready-made family in the community who not only are ready to accept your gift but who are so happy that you're here.

Meet Parisa...

I'm Parisa, I'm twenty-eight, nearly twenty-nine, so I'm getting on now! My pronouns are she/her, and I'm gay, like, fully gay. All for the girls.

I really struggled coming out, first because of my family. They were super, super anti 'it'. I remember my dad once said to me that he'd rather I came home pregnant than be gay. My dad's Persian, and in his culture being gay is the thing that you just don't do. Second, I was in my band, Only the Young, off the back of *The X Factor*, and there wasn't ever, or ever going to be, a conversation about coming out. Everyone knew. My management knew, my bandmates knew, but everyone else on the outside didn't, so I kept it quiet. I used to sneak girls into my hotel after gigs, putting coats over their heads with the help of my bandmates, which is mad! We're talking about the year 2015 or so, and it just wasn't how it is today. There weren't as many *out* gays then, especially girls. You had Sam Smith and stuff, but for girls, it wasn't a thing.

When I was in the band, I knew that all of my fans were gay. I would see on Twitter a lot of people would say things like, 'That girl's definitely gay. The brunette one's a hundred per cent gay. I'm getting gay vibes.' People still say it to me now on my TikToks; they're like, 'You gave me gay panic when I was watching you on The X Factor.' And it's so funny because it was obvious that I was, but also not obvious. If you're gay, you would know, but actually, to the broader world, sometimes they just can't see it.

I remember being in the studio and there was this dancer, and I proper, *proper* fancied her. But even then, I didn't know for sure that I was gay because I couldn't be out. So I was like, 'Am I gay? Do I fancy her?' And I absolutely did, I was obsessed! But then I would get with a boy for the sake of getting with a boy, which would gross me out now.

I've been with my partner, Poppy, for nearly six years now and we've been engaged for three. She had to deal with my family for the first two years, which was really awful. They wouldn't talk to her; I would have to go see my family without her, and she stayed with me through that time. It took me a while to stand up for her in the way that I should have done from the beginning, and I think had she not held on, we probably wouldn't be together now. It just shows how incredible she is as a person. It was really, really tough on our relationship to begin with, but I think the growth and support that we have for each other is what's kept us together. She's been my rock through everything and vice versa.

I get a bit of stick for not talking a huge amount about being queer online. But I don't live my life like that. For me, normality is the most important thing, because I spent so many years not being able to do that. Life is very different for me nowadays because I can openly talk about my partner, I can hold hands with my partner and I can just live a life with my partner and it not be a secret. Every single one of my relationships until the age of twenty-three was a secret, and that's really hard.

I think I learned how *not* to be in a relationship from my parents. From the age of sixteen I was thrust into the world of TV, and you naturally have so many issues that come with that. Personal issues, confidence issues and just hiding all of this stuff. I think because I spent so long being something for everyone else that when I met Poppy and found my person, I thought, I'm not going to apologize for it any more.

Parisa Tarjomani

As you've just read, you can see just how different and yet similar our experiences can be when it comes to coming out. I hope the different stories shared from other wonderful queer humans throughout this book show you that regardless of your journey and the opinions of those around you, they don't have to define you for the rest of your life. You can come out at any age. Doing the right thing for you to live a happy queer life may have its challenges to begin with, but I hope that you can see that with patience and self-love there is so much happiness out here waiting for you.

I'm extremely privileged to have been accepted without question by my family, although I think they always knew I was going to live life my own way from a young age. My dad, as a Scotsman who came from a very white, straight and conservative background, has accepted and even leaned in to learning about the LGBTQ+ community in a way that makes me proud to be his daughter. This is his perspective:

It doesn't feel like it's been as long as it has been that Helen has been living openly as a lesbian. But when we look back on all the occasions we've shared, it is a good indication that we've never once found it a problem.

At the time Helen broke the news I hadn't lived with her mum for a few years, so I wasn't aware of Helen not being in touch with Jacqueline, and the phone call from her mother was the first I knew of her sexuality. I wasn't in the least fazed by it though, and my first reaction was, 'Well, we don't have to worry about her coming home pregnant!' I'm not sure how much of a shock it was, I really can't remember, but her boyfriends were always more on the feminine side, so if we had thought carefully then the signs might well have been there. It most certainly never gave me pause, and I believe we have never wished for her to be anything other than herself.

I come from a small village with a village mentality, but I like to think I'm a 'live and let live' kinda guy. Over the years, I've met and mingled with lots of lesbian and gay people, both Helen's friends and my own, and have treated them all as people. I take the odd photograph when Helen needs it done and have been to lots of events, including an event for LGBTQ+ influencers at the Gay Star News offices in East London. And one year, I went to Liverpool Pride with Helen and my other (straight) daughter and we all enjoyed a fabulous day there.

The rainbow symbol is certainly accurate; colourful is an understatement within the community. It has always been a pleasure to meet her friends, and, to the best of my knowledge, I haven't caused anyone offence. If anything, it has been more interesting having a lesbian daughter. Her mum and I agree that so long as Helen is happy in herself and with herself, it's all we could wish for. We are in contact in some way or another every few days and there's rarely a month goes by when we don't meet up for something or other.

Most of all, I would say that we have the same father–daughter relationship as any other family. Helen needs shelves putting up...call dad. I've moved house for her three times in the past two years. Why would I want Helen to be something other than herself? It only makes us love her even more.

When you haven't told anybody yet, you might think of coming out as one grand gesture, but in reality it's more of a long-term practice. There will always be new people in your life and new experiences, and whether you choose to share your gift with those around you is your choice. Just know that every time you open up, it becomes less and less scary, and you're gaining a deeper love and sense of respect for your queer self, ever living in authenticity, which makes life so beautiful.

I'll finish this chapter with a thought for parents, teachers or any adult in a position of authority who might be here to learn, and the first thing I'd like to say is well done. The fact you're reading this is testament to your character. Your job is to raise and nurture humans to be the very best that they can be, to keep them safe, make them feel loved and important and to give them space and confidence to grow into their own being. It's a tough one! And whilst, yes, you have a right to care for the safety and happiness of those in your care, please do think so carefully about the impact that your thoughts and decisions have. The more you give those you care for a platform to be exactly who they are, the more you will see them flourish and grow. Sexuality, after all, is irrelevant to a person's kindness, integrity, successes and achievements. Those are the things that should be focused on, because who that person you're helping to raise ends up loving is *their* choice. And should you be lucky enough to be around to witness their love? What a gift that is.

Chapter 3

You Don't Look Like a Lesbian?

esbians, I could talk about them all day. I mean, it's a good job I'm writing a book about them, right? But let me ask you, what do you immediately think of when you hear the word lesbian? There's no right or wrong answer here, and I'm aware that even as a lesbian or queer person your first thought might be to skip to a stereotype, a derogatory word or, like me, vaginas. I'm sorry! I love 'em. My point is, each of us has a different feeling about the label depending on our personal experiences, and lordy lord I know it's not always an easy one to work with.

The word lesbian has been used *against* us rather than simply to *describe* us for so long now that a lot of us are adopting 'queer' more and more because it feels easier, less 'severe' if you like, and I totally get it. The recent reclamation of the word queer is incredibly empowering and it is now a wonderfully validating term to use on the daily. Sometimes if I'm in a rush, if I don't know someone that well or if it's just in passing, I've referred to myself as gay because it feels a little 'friendlier', safer maybe, than dropping the L bomb. But the thing is, if we strip away what we've been taught to feel about the word lesbian, and if we stop giving a shit about making the homophobes uncomfortable, then we could take it back and reclaim it just as we successfully did with the term 'queer'. Because that's what we're doing by not calling a spade a spade; we're letting the homophobes get off scot-free by putting their feelings ahead of our own and ahead of being our authentic selves. Why should we do that? I know that for most it's for fear of judgement or even violence and so, yes, in some cases it's easier and safer to just pass under the gaydar without making a peep. But in those instances where we can, if we don't start saying lesbian with our chests out, the word will be lost forever and the straight people will have won. And we can't have that. Even if just because I'm a terribly sore loser, and I don't want you to lose either. I've passed you the baton, now it's up to you to run with it as fast and hard as you bloody can.

Once you've come to the conclusion that you are, in fact, a raging lesbian, there are so many exciting facets of lesbianhood that you'll come to discover. From what you wear, who you're friends with and what type of sex you enjoy to whether you're a Fletcher fan or not (I mean it's mandatory, tbh). No, but really, there's a whole lifestyle just waiting for you to discover that is so exciting you'll look at your straight sisters and think, poor you. Yes, poor them for not getting to experience the kind of uplifting, soul-gratifying, mind-blowing feeling of living a queer life. That was what my first few months of being out felt like, being lifted up and shown what heaven looked like, and I'm telling you, all the angels are lesbians.

We're not actually going to discuss labels specifically just yet; we'll get into them properly later on in the book and the importance, or unimportance, of them depending on who you are. When discovering where you fall in the queer space, who your peers are and where you might fit, I believe we all use labels, whether you realize you're doing it or not. And so in this chapter I'm using labels, or more so categories, educationally, to help us to understand ourselves. Just take them with a pinch of salt for now and try to see the context of each label in as broad a sense as possible.

stereotype

/ˈstɛrɪə(ʊ)tʌɪp/

noun

1. A widely held but fixed and oversimplified image or idea of a particular type of person or thing.

As a young person, I grew up in a very stereotypically 'female' way. I had long, blonde hair, I loved to sing and dance, I wore skirts to school and by the time I was a teenager, I had a real passion for fashion. At fifteen I idolized Carrie Bradshaw from *Sex and the City* (if you know, you know). She was everything I wanted to be. Hyper-feminine, sexy and funny with a shoe collection that spanned a lifetime of purchases. I was utterly obsessed with her and would flip through my monthly *Vogue* magazine subscription with fervour, soaking up the creativity, the colours and, also, the models. Oh, the models. Looking back I understand that whilst, yes, the fashion was feeding my soul, it was the models who wore the clothes that I was falling in love with. Baby gay realness.

I became particularly obsessed with a model called Agyness Deyn. She was tall and had a short pixie crop, a strong jawline and heavy-set brows. She was feminine and yet masculine, and I'd never seen anyone like her before in my life. I had no real understanding of gender outside of the binary then. The term non-binary wasn't part of the wider vocabulary yet, and even the word androgynous was something I had to explain to my mum. But I was so fascinated with her. So much so that every image I could find of her was cut out, stuck into my scrapbook and eventually montaged into wallpaper that covered all four of my bedroom walls (now *that*'s lesbianism for you!).

At the time I felt like I was surrounding myself with fashion, whereas now I can see that I was surrounding myself with androgynous women who I would eventually understand to be 'my type'. But even more than that, I can see that it began to open up my mind as to how or what a woman should look like and dress like and how she should present herself to the world. Maybe my inner lesbian was giving myself a helping hand in exploring my sexuality in a way, but regardless, it certainly led me to broaden my idea of gender beyond what I had been taught, and to appreciate and really champion those who didn't confine themselves to it. To not box people up by way of their appearance and to seek out the broader intricacies beyond the stereotypes we so easily and quickly judge upon.

If there was one stereotype in the world that is the definition of its meaning, an oversimplified idea, it's that all lesbians have short hair, wear masculine style clothing, have tattoos and piercings, and/or wear an array of caps. This is probably the most well-known and well-used stereotype about lesbian women.

Now sure, (thankfully) there *are* a bunch of women around the world who absolutely love and lean into this aesthetic. This is what feels authentic to them and this is who they are.

I find stereotypes tend to be based on an element of truth so, yes, a large portion of those masc-presenting women will be lesbians. But I mean, come on! There are eight billion people in the world, and I don't know how anyone with a legitimate amount of brain cells can truly believe that all of the lesbians that exist on the planet wear lumberjack shirts and have a Justin Bieber circa 2010 haircut. You'll find that throughout this book I'll repeatedly thank the power of social media, because without it we may never get the chance to banish this stereotype because, unless we can *see* diversity with our own eyes, how do we prove this to be untrue?

My cannonball launch into the LGBTQ+ world back in 2007 saw me dive headfirst into a gay scene where I was one of very few femme lesbians. In fact, back then I was told, as a newbie, that I was a lipstick lesbian. A lesbian who favours a glamorous and traditionally feminine style. Frankly, I was the poster girl for it in my hometown. No one else was dressing in sequin hotpants and a pink wig to go to their local gay bar; I was much more like the drag queens that performed in them. All around me were butch lesbians, stem lesbians, those who have long hair but would never wear dresses type lesbians, and I wasn't taken seriously by any of them. No one believed that I was even gay at first. It was as if I was some sort of unicorn. A hyper-feminine lesbian? I couldn't be real. Remember, we don't know what we can't see, which is why representation is so incredibly important. Even by the lesbians around me, I wasn't really accepted.

As humans we have an inherent need and desire to be part of a tribe, to be surrounded by people who not only think and feel like we do, but who look like us, too. It's human nature. So the rebuttal of my peers and not having any femme gals to associate with put a little worm in my ear that maybe I should 'butch up a bit'. I was also sick of not being approached by women because they thought that I was straight, and thought that if I had a bit of a 'gay edge' I might turn a few more heads. Yes, your gal wanted to get laid! I was so keen to fit in, to be accepted and to feel 'part of the community', and so in search of my tribe, I made a decision.

My long, blonde hair fell to the floor with the buzz of a razor and I felt an instant surge of masculinity. I looked in the mirror at my bleach-blonde pixie crop and finally understood how Ruby Rose feels. Breezy about the neck but super powerful. My new look was a vibe, and in mere moments I felt so liberated. I had made the decision to cut my hair, yes, because I wanted to be 'part of the gang', but it also felt like an incredible way to mark this change in my identity outwardly to the world. I was really saying, 'Hey, I'm gay and I'm proud of it!'

At the time, I was only exposed to the small (but thriving) queer scene around me in my physical world by way of understanding what the queer aesthetic was. What lesbians looked like, what they wore, how they acted and interacted with one another. It's something you only notice or know about if you're queer. It's a feeling, an energy, and immersing yourself in it only helps to evolve your understanding of queer identity. Before being gay was decriminalized, if you wanted to find other gay people you would have to signify that by what you wore. It's called queer signalling and has been around for decades, if not centuries. In the 70s, for example, predominantly gay men signalled to one another using a handkerchief system. They would put hankies in their back pockets or their waistbands, and different coloured handkerchiefs signalled a specific sexual preference or kink. We've always found ways to find and connect with one another. I'm just so grateful that we can do that now with the tap of a few buttons on our phones.

For a few years I rocked that cropped haircut and I leaned into a more pared-down femininity, and it certainly diversified my interactions with the community I was in. And whilst I don't encourage you to change how you dress to fit in, I have to forgive my lesbian peers of the past because, like I've said before, we didn't have the visible diversity that we have today and so were uneducated on what lesbians should 'look like'. Throughout my twenties I continued to experiment with my style and had a lot of fun just letting my aesthetic evolve. I'd be influenced by trends, celebrities and people that I fancied and have learned to appreciate the power of clothing and how it can make you feel. The more confident I became in myself, the less I cared about how others perceived me or whether I looked 'gay enough' to belong there. Until now, when my sense of self is what makes me feel connected to the community, rather than whether I'm 'passing' or not. I know who I am, and I own it.

Not all of us go through a huge style evolution when we come out, and it's not mandatory to do so. Whether we're butch, femme or somewhere in the middle, we're often judged by what we look like. If you're more masc presenting, people assume you have more masculine personality traits and vice versa for femmes. But of course this is another stereotype, and one that makes me laugh as a feminine woman who dates predominantly masc-presenting women because it's usually me who wears the trousers! More on gender stereotyping in a moment, but I just want to hit it home that there is no look, no personality trait and no one way that sums up lesbianism. It's truly a rainbow-like spectrum filled with so many beautifully different possibilities and outcomes, and wherever you find yourself sitting on that spectrum is exactly where you're meant to be.

Stepping into my own aesthetic was a journey for me, as you just heard, but one that I'm so passionate about because I fully understand the power that a fabulous outfit holds. When we love what we wear, our confidence skyrockets and we become the best version of ourselves. However, we're not all born with Tan France-level styling skills, and it's not always easy to ask friends for guidance, especially if you're newly out and trying to figure out what you like. So these are the steps I would take to help settle into or to figure out your queer aesthetic:

- Pinterest – It's one of my favourite places to go for style inspiration. Start by looking at your favourite celebrities or influencers and make note of some of the items of clothing that pop up regularly so that when you're shopping, you can try those pieces for yourself.

- Thrifting – When you want to try out new styles, rather than buying new, why not try out those pieces at a fraction of the price, first? Also, thrift shops are usually full of such a variety of clothing that even just using them as a dressing-up box to play around with different styles can be useful, too.

- Be open minded – In the past, I've helped people evolve their style aesthetic (mainly girlfriends, yes; I love a fixer upper) and they look at me with a death stare when I show them an item of clothing they'd never have considered themselves. But more often than not, once you try something on, it's totally different to what you thought it might look like and what you end up liking can take you by surprise.

- Get out of the sweatpants – Look, if that's your vibe, there's no judgement from me! I have more pairs than I'm comfortable sharing, tbh. But trust me when I tell you there is no better feeling than when you put on an item of clothing that fits you perfectly, has great tailoring and isn't designed for chilling around the house in. Try to find at least one great pant suit, dress or even pair of jeans that make that ass look great. It's incredible how your self-esteem soars when you dress the part.

Remember, in everything that we do we're striving to love ourselves and to grow in confidence so that we can lead a full and happy life. It's not about making your sexuality your main personality trait, it's about being authentically you *regardless* of your sexuality, and I truly believe that taking control of and owning how you present yourself to the world can help immensely with that. There will be many people reading this who 'look gay' and many who 'don't', and whilst I love the fact that I'm gay and shout about it all day long, it's really one of the least interesting things about me, and the same goes for you. I want you to go away from reading this book feeling confident in how you look, dress, feel and love, because you're absolutely beautiful, handsome and simply gorgeous in your own unique way.

Meet Penelope...

My name is Penelope Gwen, my pronouns are she/her and I identify as bisexual.

I remember being called a lesbian in primary school and it being a very negative thing. I was attracted to certain styles, like having really short hair, so I was a bit different to the other girls at school in the aesthetics that I gravitated towards. I was quite affectionate and loving towards my friends, so I think that was the first inkling that I might be a little bit different.

In my teens I liked a girl at school and there had been this tension between us. I remember just thinking about her a lot, and one time at a sleepover we had a little moment behind the sofa but didn't kiss or anything. Sometime later, I'd left that school and I messaged her online to ask if she felt the same way and, it was absolutely mortifying, because her mom read her messages, replied and shut me down. She told me, 'Don't say this to my daughter,' like it was something very wrong. So yeah, that happened! And it was just horrific.

Another small rejection at college made me feel nervous to explore anything or to go out of my way to meet girls, so I didn't feel a part of the queer community then. I ended up in relationships with men, which also became an issue because then I'd be fetishized by them and then bisexuality would become this thing that was for their pleasure rather than mine. So something that I talk about a lot now is that you don't need to have a threesome just because you fancy girls. It's not for him. It's yours. I feel like it's expected that you have a certain promiscuity, that you like to have a lot of sex with a lot of partners and you're up for anything, which just isn't true for most.

I've also experienced men saying things like, 'It doesn't count with a woman,' and as I've gotten older I've thought 'Well why is that? Do you not see them as a threat?' There's certain outdated views and stigmas around it and, in one instance, I actually had feelings for a woman when I was with a guy. Then the jealousy came in, and they realized that women are people, are sexual beings that you could also fall in love with.

I'm now in my most successful relationship ever and it's with a woman. I don't know whether that's just by chance, and maybe I'm a little bit biased because this is going so well and I'm a little bit older than I was in previous relationships. But it's very different to what I've experienced before and the dynamic is different, sex is different, the emotional depth got there a lot quicker. It's kind of like having a best friend as well as a partner, which you can only get so much with a man, I've found. Initially I was really nervous to tell her that I was bisexual and remember thinking, 'I need to tell her because she might expect me to be a lesbian and maybe she won't like that I'm bi.' I thought maybe she wouldn't take me seriously. Thankfully it was fine, but there was definitely a feeling of 'Maybe I don't belong here?' and feeling like a little baby in this big, queer world.

When I talk about these things, a lot of people really relate to them and especially people who don't maybe feel seen or who feel how I used to feel. Visibility gives people that sense of belonging and of being a part of a community. It's important to understand how we can relate to each other, how we can relate to lesbians, to trans people. We all have similarities and are part of a much bigger thing. I'm just really grateful for where I'm at now and for being in a very healthy relationship, and looking back and being like, 'Wow, I've come so far!'

Penelope Gwen

Remembering to take labels with a pinch of salt, let's dive into some of the terms some lesbians might use to describe themselves when you're out there in the big, gay world. Whilst we're at it, let's break down and discuss some of the stereotypes or myths associated with each of them.

THE FEMME/LIPSTICK

Renowned for being the most feminine presenting of the lesbian community, think lipstick, heels and lacy lingerie. Their nightstands tend to be filled with skincare, hair grips and fashion magazines.

Stereotype/myth: All femmes are pillow princesses.

First, a pillow princess is someone who, during sex, lays back and doesn't do much other than receive. You'll find that femmes, more often than not, are not only active participants in the bedroom but can be extremely dominant. They're also, for the majority, not going to replace your mother or do all of the household chores and wash your knickers for you just because they look like a 'woman'.

THE BUTCH/MASC

On the opposite end of the lesbian spectrum, think masculine style clothing, Calvin Kleins for days, minimal make up and often short/styled-up/braided hair. Tattoos and or piercings are often part of this aesthetic, along with large collections of trainers and many, many rings.

Stereotype/myth: They're the man in the relationship.

I don't know why it's so hard for people to understand that *there is no man* in a lesbian relationship. I've personally found that butch or masc-presenting lesbians tend to be hard on the outside and soft and squidgy on the inside. But ultimately, personality isn't determined by the aesthetic you have. As humans, butch and masc-presenting women or queer people want to be treated to a date night just as much as anyone else.

THE STEM/SOFT BUTCH/CHAPSTICK

Sitting somewhere in the middle of the masc–femme scale, this could include long or short hair, a mixture of masc/femme styling and could slide more one way than the other depending on mood.

Stereotype/myth: They're non-binary.

Whilst this could be a safe haven for non-binary people in terms of aesthetic, not all ChapStick lesbians are, or will identify as, non-binary, of course. This in-between space in terms of style gives people so much room to discover how different types of clothing can make them feel. Playing around with both masc and feminine style clothing is, quite simply, hot.

THE STUD

A butch woman or a non-binary person who is of Black or Latinx descent. Only Black and Latinx women or non-binary people can use this term as it's a part of their culture.

Stereotype/myth: All masc presenting Black women use the 'stud' label.

A lesson for those who are new to the queer space, but also for the community at large, too: a Black woman or non-binary person can be masc-presenting and not identify as a stud, and yet they may do. It's really down to personal choice and feeling and certainly shouldn't be assumed simply because someone is Black. As with pronouns, gender and sexuality, never assume to know before you're told.

THE COTTAGECORE

A label that only makes sense to those who immerse themselves in queer culture, cottagecore started out as a fashion aesthetic celebrating an idealized rural life. But because queer people are cute and funny and care about the planet we adopted it because, well, if the shoe fits! Masc or femme, they grow their own vegetables and most likely have a variety of pets.

Stereotype/myth: They're all vegans.

Now if I'm totally honest, I've never met a cottagecore lesbian who isn't one! But of course, we're all unique in our own ways and we're no longer generalizing these days, okay?

As much as lesbian labels or categories have an element of truth to them, in general women and non-binary people are feeling more and more empowered to dress however they please, and it's really the next generation coming through that are proving that. There's less adversity to 'looking like a lesbian' because of TikTokers who are championing their sexuality in all its glory and cultivating huge followings simply for being themselves. Women in particular are realizing they don't have to 'look feminine' to identify as one, and there's such power among us now because we have the opportunity to see other people who look like us regardless of our style or aesthetic. Likewise, the younger generation have been instrumental in creating a broader range of terminology to describe themselves. Just look at the introduction of pronouns, or the Mx identification on passports (for those who are non-binary). They've not only accepted but indulged in their nuances and decided that the English language needed to do better. It's benefited all of us, and I'm so here for it!

So we know that queerness doesn't have just one look, but universally there is *something* that tells you that another person is gay. It's hard to put into words because it's not an item of clothing or a hair or eye colour, but lesbians and queer women just have a *vibe* about them. I know that's not the most helpful thing in the world, but the more you're around lesbians, the more you start to just 'get it'. From masc to femmes and everything in between, there's something about our aura that shouts 'Queer!' But what do you do if your gaydar is broken?

gaydar
/ˈɡeɪdɑː/
noun INFORMAL
1. The supposed ability of gay people to recognize one another by means of very slight indications.

Sometimes it's easy to spot if someone is queer. They might be displaying the rainbow flag openly, have a pronoun badge on or be working behind the bar at a gay club. Some, at least likely, telltale signs that they might be in our club. But like I say, sometimes it's just a vibe, and so this is where we fall upon our ancestors' techniques of queer signalling. How on earth do we know if the hot person we're crushing on sitting opposite us in the coffee shop is gay, too? Well, here are some of things I would be looking out for:

- Short nails – There are definitely lesbians out there with long nails, hell I rock an acrylic every now and again, but for the most part we tend to keep our nails short for, well, y'know! They could be painted, manicured, everyone is different, but I have to say the rise in lesbians of all style aesthetics indulging in nail art of late has been cute af. You do you, boo! Regardless of whether they're painted or not, most lesbians generally keep them short. There's a whole conspiracy theory surrounding lesbian hands having a certain 'look' to them, but I'll leave you to get into your own TikTok black hole on that one!

- Thumb ring – Lesbians have adopted the thumb ring as a symbol of their queerness for some time now. It's become universally known that the thumb ring is ours, so if you don't have one on, what are you waiting for? Style-wise it's generally a simple band, but I've always been sure to flash mine when spotting someone I fancy. The thumb ring is so inherently gay that my first girlfriend gave me one and I've not taken it off in seventeen years.

- Are they following Fletcher? – This was a joke when I first typed it out, but actually getting a good idea of who someone follows on social media is a pretty good indicator of whether they're queer or not. If they're following Kehlani, JoJo Siwa or any of the cast of *The L Word*, I think we're good! Either they're gay, or an incredible ally!

- Out yourself – Scary, but the most effective. If all else fails, go ahead and out yourself, creating a safe space for them to either out themselves too or for you to stand corrected. Regardless of their response, it's always a good icebreaker to make someone feel safe to be their authentic selves with you, too.

There's so many more of these; the lesbian nod, the way someone sits, their music choices, whether they have cats or not. That can all help to build a picture of whether or not someone is queer. I say, be bold in your pursuit of spotting queer siblings out and about in the world, and remember, you can't judge a book by its cover, so always lead with an open mind and you never know who you might bump into.

Today, thankfully, there are more and more 'safe spaces' for queer people to get together, meet one another and to be themselves and so we don't necessarily need to be subtle with our signalling any more. We're about to dive into how we go about finding our queer peers in the next chapter, and it's one of my favourites to help you on this incredibly exciting queer journey. Sadly, however, there are still sixty-nine countries around the world where being LGBTQ+ is illegal, and eleven of those countries still impose the death penalty. I bring that up as just another reason for my encouraging you to live a full life, because there are so many who can't or won't get the opportunity to. Be thankful and true for them, be out and proud for those people, because I'm sure that given a chance, they would trade places with you in a heartbeat.

As for lesbian stereotypes, or finding your lesbian aesthetic, I don't think we're out of the woods just yet. There'll always be people out there who are quick to judge or who can't quite get their heads around those who choose to dress or express themselves differently to what they're used to, but that's the same with anything. There'll always be someone out there judging you whatever you choose to do, so why not be yourself anyway and let them deal with it? As long as you love and accept you, that's fine by me. Masc, femme, stem, whatever! A lesbian's a lesbian in my eyes, and a bloody gorgeous one.

Chapter 4

Discovering Your Second Family

I was seventeen, had just discovered I was a lesbian and was in total awe of this new, rainbow-coloured world that had opened up to me. As often as I could, I'd be out, partying the night away in gay bars and immersing myself in queer culture. I read *Diva* magazine, gathered a posse of gay boys around me and I listened to Missy Higgins on repeat (the Fletcher of the noughties). I watched *Lip Service* (the old school *The L Word*) and crushed hard on Kate Moennig like every femme lesbian had done before me. I felt so right about how my life had changed. I felt so *me*.

I mentioned in the previous chapter that whilst, yes, I was walking the walk of my baby gay self and loving every second of it, I really struggled to connect with other queer women. First, there weren't a lot of femme lesbians around that I could shoe shop with, and when there were, they were worried I was out to steal their woman (don't test me, hon). So the friendship group that I enveloped myself in I would class as the alternative gays, the misfits, the black sheep of the community. It was always fun and I had an abundance of people I could call last minute to go try out a new gay bar, but I knew, even then, that a lot of these friendships would be transient. That it was going to take me some time to find 'my people', and that these early relationships and friendships would ebb and flow just like everything else in life.

The local gay bars had become what my new life was centred around, and now that I was in it, I was addicted. My average week would look like this: Tuesdays, Bar 131 for urban/RnB vibes. Wednesdays, karaoke at local gay hangout Colors. Thursdays, Smiths Bar in Chelmsford for cocktails and power lesbians. Fridays, Colors club night with a drag queen thrown in for good measure. Saturdays, The Cliff pub followed by Hush gay bar for ultimate pop hits and Gold-schläger. Sundays, Chicago's in Chelmsford for a guaranteed snog. Mondays, have a rest, babe, before you kill yourself! There was something fun to do every night of the week where I grew up, but it was Sundays that I and the rest of the queer people in my home county lived for. 'Chi-gay-go's' we called it, and they were wild, wild times. The club had a corridor for an entrance that opened out onto a raised platform where you overlooked the entire club. You'd walk down the steps into the club itself and everyone in the room could see you enter. It was nerve-wracking, actually, but it was your chance to scour the room before heading straight to the bar and the night would begin!

Back then I was experiencing so many new things and had such a busy social life so I never consciously dwelled on my lack of like-minded pals. We were all gay and just wanted to be out partying and having fun and that felt like a good enough connection at that point. But sometimes I craved something deeper with someone who understood what being a 'lipstick lesbian' was like and the experiences that I was having. Had social media been a more prolific tool in connecting communities back then, I would have been able to find my kin, no problem. You can type in the hashtag #femmelesbian to TikTok and we're all there, doing the absolute most (you're welcome). However, with the rise of the internet, all of those gay bars that I was going to – a night out for every day of the week – are gone. The places we can gather, meet, party and connect in person are diminishing one by one. Frankly we've become too busy making online connections and so gays bars simply can't sustain themselves with fewer regular customers. Lifestyle choices and the cost of living makes it harder for us to have a thriving social life these days, too.

The lack of queer spaces is a sad issue and a really important one because human connection is more vital than ever. We've discussed how crucial representation is and how life changing and honestly, life*saving* it is to be able to go to a queer space and immerse yourself in the community. It's hard to rally us all together when our wants and needs are so carefully catered for in our online worlds. Each letter of the acronym has its own ideas of what a night out looks like, and within those acronyms we all have different personal tastes too, and so with the power of choice, queer spaces find it harder and harder to find a sizeable enough audience to run a feasible business. Nowadays, rather than gay bars we have queer events. Lesbian nights, queer nights, gay nights that are either monthly or that tour around, hitting different cities that you have to travel to. There *is* importance in having events that cater to who you are specifically, but it's a sad loss that there are fewer and fewer consistent safe spaces where, regardless of how you identify, you're welcome and you belong and you can be surrounded by community.

And so although without the internet I only had the

people of Essex to liken myself to, I don't wish that time of my life to be any different. I don't wish I'd had the internet in my early years to find my femme pals sooner because, not to rub it in, I got to live through the height of queer party culture and I wouldn't trade it for the world. It was such an important time in my life to be surrounded by my peers and I think it helped me to accept and revel in who I was. The contradiction to that being that without the internet, I may not have met some of my closest friends, people who have changed my life and helped me to be my most honest and true self. Would I ever have met those people irl? Who knows. And how could I not mention that it's the internet that meant I was able to meet my current girlfriend? Yes, babes, she slid into my DMs.

Having lived through both worlds, the age of no social media and now having an abundance of it, I can confidently say that there's not one way, or a *right* way, of finding your queer peers (I love that that rhymes). If anything, we're more able to find people with specific interests, thoughts and feelings similar to our own because the entire human race has been opened up to us. For the most part, the internet has given us a broader understanding of diversity in the human race and has solidified the idea that being part of the LGBTQ+ community is valid. It's abundantly obvious that we're here, we're queer and we're not going anywhere. And so with the tools that we have at our fingertips of finding connection in community, how do we go about doing that?

When I came out, I was surrounded by straight girls and gay boys at a performing arts school, and whilst I never experienced any extreme homophobia there, the more I stepped into my queer identity outside of college, the more isolated I felt showing up to class every day. It's extremely difficult being surrounded by people and yet feeling totally isolated at the same time, and if you've suffered with your mental health, you'll know the feeling. There were multiple issues I was battling within that environment: it was very competitive, I was the youngest student in my year group and whilst mature, was still developing into adulthood. Then of course, I'd come out as a lesbian, in a space full of very straight, white women, and I add 'white' to showcase a real lack of diversity in *any* shape or form. It was tough. I felt very 'other' walking into that building every day, which is why I was so grateful for, and felt most alive, in my social life. That's where I could really be my authentic self.

Back in 2007, mental health wasn't discussed as it is today; it wasn't a factor of daily life that people took into account, but I can see now that I was very sad and angry during that period of my life. Being one person by day and another by night is a strange dual life to lead, and it affected me to the point that I really struggled to make any friends in college. I probably wasn't the easiest person to try to make friends *with*, but I feel like there was a real lack of care by the adults, teachers and faculty to help a seventeen-year-old girl struggling with her identity and sense of self. Maybe back then we just weren't as equipped as we are now, but thank god for the queer friends I surrounded myself with outside of college because without them, I don't know how things would have played out.

This is why I'm such an advocate for finding community and friends *in real life*. I've been one person in one space and someone else in another, and the internet is the most likely place you can replicate that behaviour. In some ways, the internet might be the only place where you can be yourself when you first discover your sexuality or are dabbling with it. But if you spend too long there, you can very easily isolate yourself in the real world. It's an incredible tool for finding like-minded individuals, but it's also a place that breeds comparison and where people tend to show you only the best bits of their lives. You never know how happy you can be in the moment until you put your phone down and connect with people one on one. Doing that is one of the most important things I want you to do, so let's get serious about making queer pals of the physical kind.

One day, I was sitting in the cafeteria at college, alone (I told you I had no mates), when a girl came in and struck up a conversation with me. We were chatting about what we'd been up to that weekend when she casually slipped into conversation that she was gay, too! Now if you ever find yourself in the position where you're the only gay in the village, which can happen quite a lot, at school, in the workplace, where you live or in your family, when you find another queer, regardless of where they fall on the spectrum, it's like winning fifty pounds on a scratch card. It's such a life-affirming feeling, a sense of belonging and understanding of what the other person feels and has potentially been through. It's a beautiful feeling.

From that conversation we became fast friends and spent the last two years of college life joined at the hip. We went out together, performed together, went through break ups together and shared so many incredible memories. She was feminine, bisexual and a performer like me, and it was such an affirmation of my queerness. I needed that more than I knew at the time, and I could finally see that it didn't matter how I dressed, what I did for a living, my hair length or the way I was raised. I was gay and I was valid. Your straight friends can support and love you and that's important too, to have allies around you, but having a queer network is irreplaceable for your head and heart.

I've gone through so many different phases of friendships throughout my life, from my girl gang at school to my college friends and then to the pals I made when my marriage broke down (more on that later), and having these different people enter and then have some leave my life is perfectly normal. We're not really taught that, just like romantic relationships, friendships don't always last a lifetime either, and it's time that narrative was put to bed. We change so much as we grow into ourselves and then continue to evolve the older we get, and different people and friendships serve different times in our lives. Friendships can naturally fizzle out, trust can be broken, people change and we can simply fall out of sync with friends too as we grow. The cycle of life and who you spend time with is ever evolving, but all of the experiences that you have are beneficial, are worthwhile and will teach you different life lessons along the way.

These days I'm very choosy with who I spend real, quality time with and have a mixture of queer and straight pals to keep me busy. I call these people my chosen family, because I feel blessed to know them and to have them in my life in such a close way. My best friend and right arm, Fran, is so straight she puts rulers to shame, but is the most amazing ally you could meet. Even in my thirties I'm adding to my second family all of the time, with people like Lucy London, who I met in my late twenties and now can't live without, and my favourite power couple, Nic and Ruth, who again, I met fairly recently but have shared some of my most treasured memories with. It's important to take time to connect with people in the flesh; nothing compares to sitting next to someone or looking into a friend's eyes when they're talking and to pass energy to and fro with someone you love and who cares about you in return. Just remember that who you surround yourself with is going to have a huge impact on your life, and therefore choose wisely and think carefully. There's not always a need to rush into things, like I did...

By the time I was nineteen, I had a couple of years of raucous behaviour behind me, from pulling all-nighters with women I'd just met to falling in and out of love and gallivanting off on trips to gay bars across the country. I had sincerely established my queerness and was having the time of my life growing into my own person more and more every day. I had full on lesbian swag. I had (metaphorical) balls!

I met Emily as I was graduating college. She was older than me, drove a Mercedes and had even more swag than I did. She was funny and aloof but generous and soft, and I fell in love with her quickly. For a while, long distance was our only option as I'd gotten a job performing in a seaside hotel, and so on my one day off a week, I'd get an overnight train to travel home to see her. We'd spend eight hours together and then I'd head back to the coast. It was the kind of love that made you do crazy things. Crazy things like get married.

Yes, just a few months in, Emily and I were engaged, and it was the most romantic thing that had ever happened to me. It was a whirlwind of a time and I remember longing to have the kind of stability I hadn't had as a child. My parents having separated, I craved safety in my romantic relationships. The thing is, when you mix that sort of longing with someone who's a hopeless romantic, all judgement is thrown out of the window, and this is the sort of outcome you get. Our wedding was beautiful. My nan made my wedding dress, my dad was our photographer and Lucy's parents were extremely generous, booking us a countryside manor. To top it all off, we even had drag queens perform for our guests from our favourite cabaret club in London. I remember standing in a side room moments before walking down the aisle thinking, am I really doing this?

Of course it's very possible to meet the love of your life before you hit your twenties; there's no right time to find Mrs Right, after all. But as I mentioned earlier, my marriage didn't last. Although I felt like a grown-ass woman at the time, I was just a twenty-year-old kid who knew absolutely nothing about what a healthy relationship looked like, and it would be some time before I cracked it. Since then, Emily and I have found a middle ground in a way that only lesbians can, and have a 'sort of' friendship. But back then, I was in the relationship hoping to make a family in her, looking for the stability I so craved and trying to reframe my idea of what a healthy relationship looks like. And of course, those are all fantastic ways to break up a partnership! You're probably thinking, 'Why did you do it then, Helen?' Well truthfully, I didn't see it at the time; most people don't. It wasn't until my mid-twenties and people began talking openly about mental health, about therapy and about self-growth that I would take the time to look after myself in that way.

This part of my life taught me that you can't find peace in those around you until you find peace in yourself. Cultivating your queer family goes for romantic relationships as well as friendships, and I'd just done a shoddy job of cultivating mine. It would be the first of many times that I thought to myself, 'I'm so good at friendships, but rubbish at relationships' and wondered why that was. Nowadays, I can look back and feel more tenderness towards the person I was then. I had so much unlearning and relearning to do, as a lot of us do with regards to one thing or another, and I know that I was really trying to figure my shit out. I was, however, a great queer pal to have around because I encouraged those around me to be their most authentic selves, to love themselves loudly and proudly, which I still do to this day. But on the relationship side of things, I'd grown up with this subconscious belief that love was hard won and that I wasn't worthy of it by simply existing, and so I failed in that area of my life time and time again. Thankfully a tonne of therapy and a lot of tears have helped me to shake those beliefs, but it taught me that we all have our demons, something we're battling with, and not dealing with your shit is only going to hold you back and cause you pain down the line. The more accepting and understanding you are of yourself, the more you can be objective and communicate your thoughts and feelings within yourself and with those around you, which will make it a lot easier to find those queer peers who are imperative to your well-being, whether you're marrying them or not.

Meet Rose and Nana...

I'm Rose, my pronouns are she/they and I identify as a lesbian.

My name is Nana. My pronouns are she/they and I identify as queer.

R: I was pretty young when I had my first girl-on-girl experience. I grew up as a Mormon and there was another family in the Mormon church whose children went to the school next to mine. Their parents worked night shifts and so the daughter, who was my age, would stay at my house Monday to Friday. We used to kiss and touch each other's bodies and I didn't know anything about lesbians or gay people back then, but it didn't feel like what we were doing was abnormal. We were just doing things! By secondary school, I knew what the labels were, but everybody was homophobic and there was no way that I was going to tell anyone that I was gay or bi.

N: I had this crush on my English teacher. I had just put it down to the fact that I liked English! It was my favourite subject, so I didn't think it was because I was gay but looking back on it now it was probably a bit of both. I used to think about her all the time and then it came as a light bulb moment. 'You like girls,' and that was just that. At the time, I was a Christian, and didn't have any gay role models, or specifically Black gay role models, to look up to and I thought, ignorantly, that it was a white thing. My parents would say that being gay was an English thing and that there were no gays in Africa, which is of course a total lie. But back then I actually believed that. Fast forward to uni and the feelings just started bubbling over and I couldn't ignore it at that point. I needed to find out if I was gay or not, so I slept with a guy, which was not a good thing to do. Do not sleep with a guy just to find out if you're queer!

R: You want to find out if you're a lesbian, but you sleep with a guy... Isn't that interesting? Like why did you not sleep with a girl to find out?

N: I know, right? But then I guess I wanted to rule it out!

R: Growing up as a Mormon, if I wasn't at school, I was at church. And even when I was at home, the missionaries from the church were in our house and it was just very, very religious. They would speak about the way your life was meant to be and there were no options for anything else, so I didn't think it was even possible for me. There was just no one queer who looked like me.

N: I was on Twitter in 2010 and I saw a girl who was openly tweeting about her queer sexcapades and I was like, 'Oh my god, she's gay!' So I followed her, she invited me out to a club night and it was insane; I had this out of body experience. I kept going back and it was just a safe space where it felt like everyone was being themselves basically, everyone was having fun, and it was so nice to see. I met new people from attending Pride and my friendships grew from there. It's so important because we really check in on each other, talk about things and there's a lot of care that's taken with each other.

R: Initially we wanted somebody to go to these spaces with, right? We didn't wanna go to these places by ourselves. You just want someone to hold hands with in these environments. The Black queer scene (in London) is just tiny. Everyone knew somebody and we just kind of built a friendship group from there. Some have dropped off along the way, and we've gained some people as well and I think right now we're at a very solid place.

N: Being friends with Rose has made me feel more comfortable in my own skin and it's made me feel more confident as well. We just had this connection from the jump, we have chemistry. I think when people think about chemistry they often think about romantic relationships, but you have to have chemistry in order to be friends, too. We have a very similar upbringing because we're both Ghanaian and so we can relate to each other really, really well.

We grew up in households where our parents didn't speak about their feelings or their mental health and so it's been hard for us to speak about those things because it makes us feel very, very vulnerable. And we've had to help each other come out of that and speak up about what we're going through. Gradually over time we're becoming more comfortable but we're sort of also holding each other accountable too, which I love.

Rose Frimpong and Nana Duncan

There are going to be certain types or communities of people who are going to struggle accepting your sexuality, from those with certain religious beliefs to those with certain political viewpoints. And navigating how, when and where is safe to establish your sexuality is a juggling act. Add to that the fact that the word lesbian in general isn't the easiest word to associate with, it can feel like a minefield. Right now, the word lesbian is facing a tough time, as it's been sexualized for years, and most recently, it's been attached to trans-exclusionary radical feminists (TERFs), a minority of those who describe themselves as 'feminists' but actually hold the deeply transphobic view that trans women are not women.

Trans-exclusionary radical feminists have somewhat of a lesbian following and campaign against trans inclusivity. Something they bring up continuously is their opposition to trans women using women's public bathrooms, describing, in interviews, that this is 'abolishing women's protected spaces' and stating that it's 'dangerous for women and girls' for trans women to do so. Their backing for this is that 'some men will choose to exploit the right to legally change their gender to abuse women'. Nicola Sturgeon, former First Minister of Scotland and Leader of the Scottish National Party from 2014 to 2023, responded to those concerns with this statement: 'The worry is that some men will choose to exploit that process (the right to legally change their gender) to abuse women. Most men who want to abuse women don't feel the need to change their gender to do it.' Which really derails that argument in a few short words. It's not trans women who would be causing that issue, you see? It's just so damaging, degrading and, ultimately, lethal in many cases for trans women to be the subject of debate like this. The fact that lesbians are so closely linked with TERFs does nothing to aid in the reclamation of the label; in fact, it's extremely harmful. It's excruciatingly frustrating that some lesbians are siding with this viewpoint instead of uplifting our trans sisters, who frankly already struggle to simply exist.

Then we have age-old misogyny to deal with. No, lesbians don't get away with it just because we fancy the same gender that men do. Straight men have fantasized about lesbians for centuries, diminishing their respect for female exclusive relationships and sexualizing us instead. And so we're left with the world viewing us as sordid and slutty and something to look down upon. We don't have an easy time of it at all and with such little education around sexuality and sex, there's so much misinformation spread that we just haven't had a chance to say, 'We've had enough!' It's been a bit of a shit show to be honest with you, but the more time I spend online, the more I'm seeing a wave of young people claiming the word and not being afraid to shout about it. Times are changing, and the word lesbian is one that I will champion until I die because we're human beings, here to be taken seriously, to challenge the narrative written for us, and we are certainly not sexual objects or political statements. We simply love women and, quite frankly, who can blame us?

I don't take for granted my passing appearance, meaning that to the world at large, I don't 'look' gay, and I'm also a white, blonde girl, which again, makes for an easier life than most. I know that for those in less privileged positions, it can be a much tougher experience, so having those queer siblings and safeguarding measures in place is going to be so important for your mental and physical well-being. Be intentional with who you invite into your life, and where possible, use your voice to be out and proud to encourage education and to develop a better understanding of LGBTQ+ culture for our entire community.

Now you're thinking, 'Okay, Helen, thanks for the TED Talk, babes, but how on earth am I out here making new lesbian friends?' Okay, okay, I hear you! So let's jump into the ways that you can go about finding your queer family, *other* than just on socials. Like I've said, the online world has an abundance of queer, just get your hashtags out and start searching. But I want to encourage you to create some irl friendships and connections, and the first place I'd start is on dating apps.

Most dating apps nowadays give you the option to search for platonic relationships as well as romantic ones, or at the least you're able to state that's what you're looking for in your bio. Set the search area to an appropriate travelling distance for you, and you're ready to go! You could write in your bio 'Looking to make new friends with similar interests' followed by some of the things that you enjoy and the activities you'd be open to trying. This is a great way to start making connections locally, especially if you're a little more shy or aren't out yet; just make sure that you follow through and make those plans to meet. Remember, we can't hide out on the internet, so book a coffee date, a trip to a local museum or a night out to a gay bar and make those irl connections. Whenever you're speaking to strangers online, make sure you're looking after your safety, and don't disclose personal information before you really know and trust that person, and it's also worth making your meetups in public spaces until you really know them. Otherwise jump in and get connecting; there's a world of queers waiting for that match!

Let's talk about sports. Not to be stereotypical, but let's face it, a lot of lesbians like to play sports, watch sports or talk about sports. So whether you join a team or head out to support, they're often a great way to strike up new friendships over a shared passion. Team sports often do a lot of social activities together – nights out, team bonding sessions – and are a way to make strong connections, fast. Being the newbie could put you off starting, but just get yourself to that first session, and you'll see how quickly you adapt. And look, it doesn't have to be a sport. A quick google and you're bound to find an LGBTQ+ choir, book, bird watching, swing dance, rock climbing, gaming, amateur dramatics or 'you name it' club somewhere nearby. And if all else fails and you can't find a club, team or group that speaks to what you're into, why not start your own? When you're the planner of an event, as the go-to person, it makes conversation a little easier. Plus, you'd be playing your part in creating safe spaces for the community, which would be awesome!

Get a part-time or, hell, a full-time job in an LGBTQ+ venue or workplace. Gay bars, queer-focused charities, magazines and event spaces, there's a tonne of jobs that have queerness at the heart of them. That way there's no chance you'll miss out on making new queer acquaintances by putting yourself in the heart of an already established community. If moving or changing jobs isn't an option right now, you could consider volunteer work if that's a viable option to you, for charities, Pride events or organizations that speak to you. Again, centring queerness in your life will open you up to meeting those like-minded kin we're seeking and is also extremely rewarding. Giving back and uplifting others will, in turn, boost your own self-esteem and leave you feeling fulfilled in your own skin.

Who doesn't love a night out? Okay, some people don't, actually, and each to their own! But if it *is* your thing, get searching for those queer events, clubs or bars that are within travelling distance for you. The smell in the air, the vibes, the aesthetic, it's just, chef's kiss! With everyone feeling safe, free and happy, it's one of my favourite ways to meet new people and celebrate being queer at the same time. Finding the courage to approach people is your next step, so having someone to go with can help give you a bit of confidence. And remember, vulnerability is sexy, so be upfront about your newness and if in doubt, smile it out. If going with a pal isn't an option, there's often a solos or singles WhatsApp or Telegram group that you can join for certain events to get to know people beforehand. Otherwise, get prepared with a few practised introductions, questions and topics of convo to ease the nerves. And just remember, we've all been a baby gay once. We'll go easy on you, we promise!

I want this part of your life to be filled with fun. You deserve an abundance of queer connections that set your heart alight and that encourage you to feel settled, accepted and, I hate to say it but, 'normal', because that's exactly what you are! My best friend, who I've known my whole life, is the epitome of a straight woman, but she knows me better than anyone. I then have Kel, who's bisexual and has been in my life since we were teens. Christina is a smoking hot, high-powered bisexual woman in a relationship with a wonderful man. Dr Perchard, Freddie Bentley and Daryl are flamboyantly fabulous gays that I just so happen to know, and the list of wonderful humans who I'm privileged to call friends goes on. Like me, it's not mandatory that your tribe is queer, but having those associations is only going to positively impact your life. You deserve the same rights as our straight peers, including a wild and wonderful dating life – which we're moving onto next – and it all comes back to that one important thing: connection. Take every opportunity you have to surround yourself with people who make you feel like the very best version of you, because you deserve to have a sense of belonging and to shed any negative connotations that you have or have been taught to feel. You deserve family, and there's no family so fabulous as your LGBTQ+ one.

Chapter 5

The Chaos of Dating and the Urge to Merge

Lesbians can be utter chaos. Just have a scroll online at the lesbian drama that can go down over one song like 'Becky's So Hot' by Fletcher. Iconic behaviour, but also, if it's *your* life and *your* drama, maybe it's not so fun. And so I feel like I should prepare you that, as much as I hate to say it, two women in a relationship together can be a little chaotic. Beautiful and wonderful, yes, but a roller-coaster of emotions if you're not careful. That's not to tar all lesbians with the same brush (obvs), but let's face it, women are generally very much in tune with their emotions and feelings, and so times that by two on a bad day, and all hell can break loose.

Take emotional intelligence, the ability to form close bonds with other women quickly and then add sexual tension into the mix and it can lead to all sorts of mischief. As women and queer people, we have the scope to maximize all of our relationships in different ways. As you might have seen online, lesbians can form tight-knit friendship groups with each other, or cliques if you like, which can be full of interchanging incidents, relationships and feelings. *The L Word* really has a lot to answer for. We'll get into pros and cons of lesbian cliques a little later on, but our general openness and emotional depth means that not only can our friendship groups be exciting to navigate but so too can our dating lives.

Dating to me is a bit like shopping. You walk in, excited at the possibility of what you might find, you try some things on only to find that the top doesn't fit, that jumper's nice but the wrong colour and then it's just love at first sight when you find a pair of jeans that fit you perfectly. Dating is similar in that for most of us, we have to shop around and try people on a bit before we find 'the one' that fits. I met my first girlfriend irl as you know, but over the years I've tried a plethora of different ways to meet women, to date and to experiment. I'm a 'life's too short' kind of gal, and thanks in part to my very open minded and liberal upbringing, I've always been extremely open minded and nonjudgemental when it comes to sex and dating. I don't know whether it's my inner hopeless romantic, my thirst for intimate connections and experiences, a real passion for women or all of the above. But I've always been very much in the thick of the dating scene and have truly dabbled in a bit of everything. Sex parties, throuples or nonmonogamy, you name it, I've given it a go!

I'm not saying that you should go out and do the same, but I want you to know that as long as you're not harming anyone along the way, you can have sex with and date whoever you like and enjoy any type of related activity that takes your fancy. The more experiences you have – and they can be anything from being active on dating apps to going to a swingers' party – the more you're bound to learn about yourself. It's all about listening to your head and your heart and doing exactly what you want to do. Having autonomy over your thoughts, feelings and actions. I know lots of people who have never had a one-night stand because they're very much about the intimacy and it just isn't what they enjoy. And then I know lots of people who love a one-night stand, enjoy casual sex and are happy, successful humans. Listen to yourself, communicate with yourself after every experience you have, every date, interaction, and get to know exactly where you're at so that you can make the most out of every experience.

Most humans have a type. Whether it's physical attributes that we're drawn to or certain personality traits that drive you wild, we've all got something that just 'does it' for us. I've always been more enthralled by personality than looks, but I can't deny I'm a sucker for mascs. I'm attracted to the polar opposite of me in look, and whilst I hate to be a cliche, tall, dark and handsome is my type aesthetically. The main thing that I've always looked for, though, is someone who wants to boss life with me, a partner in crime, a team mate to be there with me through thick and thin. Now *there's* the hopeless romantic in me. I haven't always gone about finding them in the right way, especially pre-therapy, when I learned that a lot of my thought processes around relationships had been somewhat unhealthy and leaned heavily on the idea of someone else bringing me happiness, rather than adding to it. It's so common, particularly in our community where we have a lot of shame around who we are, to want to be in a relationship simply to feel loved (we'll get to this in a moment).

My open attitude towards dating, sex and relationships has

meant I've been able to create and enjoy so many different incredible connections and experiences with people which have made me who I am today. Don't get me wrong, I've not always got it right, and I'll share some of my stories with you now to encourage you to see that we all make choices, good, bad and ugly, which make life the incredible journey that it is. It's up to you to make the most, or little, of it as you wish. Your way of doing things is normal for you, as long as you're not hurting others and are getting your sexual health check-ups regularly, okay?

I met a girl called Gabi on a dating app. She was Brazilian, had a great job in PR and was extremely fit. Whilst her texts were at times a little hard to decipher because of her broken English, we decided to meet for a drink at a local bar to see if our connection transferred offline. I turned up to the date only to realize that Gabi had been using Google Translate the entire time and couldn't speak a word of English. At first, I really didn't know what to do, but as someone determined to find a solution to most things, I came to find that there are fantastic ways of communicating with someone other than verbally. What also came to materialize, much to my surprise, was that Gabi was also married to a man named Luca. I had unwittingly entered a three-way relationship and although at first I was shocked, it was also a thrill to realize that three isn't always such a crowd. I couldn't understand a bloody word that was being said for the most part, but I learned very quickly that situationships like that, without the ability to properly communicate, can never last long. It also taught me the important lesson of knowing when to leave the party.

I was on my way home from work late one night in London and had gotten on the wrong train. I was sat scrolling on my phone, waiting for the next stop to be able to reroute myself, and was surprised when I heard someone call my name from down the carriage. It was a girl I'd snogged on a night out a few years earlier and let me tell you, she looked good. I took it as some sort of universal sign that we'd bumped into each other on a train that I was never supposed to get, and so I arranged a date with her. I felt like I was in a movie! However, after the date she came back to mine for a sleepover, and the universe proved to mean jack shit when my housemate had to help me forcefully remove her from the flat at three in the morning when she was frustrated that I wouldn't put out. It was, thankfully, the only experience I've had like it. But it was a stark reminder that if you're going to casually date or let people into your personal space who you don't know very well, you have to be aware of your personal safety. It's very easy to have your guard down if you're dating women or queer-identifying people, but having preventative safety measures in place are ever important, regardless.

I dated Sara for around three months or so. She was a pretty high-powered career woman with the most incredibly blue eyes, and she was extremely generous. She worked out with an online coach twice a week who was, of course, a lesbian, and we even did a couple's session together one time. Whilst Sara and I had a lot of fun together, that relationship was sadly short lived, and during my post break up glow up, I asked the same trainer if she could take me on as a client. I'm not doing myself any favours on the cliche front here and am sure you can guess what happened next – I told you I've been a right messy cow over the years – but yes. Me and the PT were obsessed with one another within weeks. What started off as a text message here and there about what the best sources of protein are led to her driving to my flat at one in the morning because we had to know what kissing each other would feel like. But Famalam, there's more. You see, the PT wasn't single. 'Why in the lesbian gods,' I hear you say, 'did you fall for a woman who wasn't available?' Well let this be a lesson to you, my loves. First, you can't always help who you fall for. I don't condone my behaviour, but sometimes you meet people in life who you have undeniable and instant chemistry with. We don't get to choose. And second, she told me they were breaking up (which of course is the biggest line you'll ever hear) and so more fool me.

As you can see, I've had quite the varied dating life. I've not been afraid to roll with things and have had a lot of fun along the way as well as learning some harsh and extremely valid lessons, too. Good dates, bad dates and everything in between, there aren't many avenues that I haven't explored, and I've actually already shared with you exactly how I'd go about jumping into dating back in Chapter 4. Those ways of meeting new pals that we delved into can be used for meeting new romantic interests, too. You just need to add a little extra...spice.

- Online dating – There's no denying that variety is the spice of life and that's exactly what dating apps afford us: variety. They broaden the pool of people available to us and should be used with intention. Remember not to give out personal information about yourself over the internet; instead, use online spaces as a stomping ground to grow your confidence, to work on your flirting skills and to figure out your type. One thing that lesbians seem to be really bad at online is making the first move. If you match with someone on a dating app, send a damn message! Don't be afraid to message first and to get the ball rolling. She'll love the confidence, I promise you.

- Use your hobbies – Again, be proactive in seeking out the gays and let the shared interests spark a romantic interest. Oftentimes when you meet someone in a group setting, the other members feel like they have some sort of stake in the relationship and can get a little too involved. So if you do meet a romantic interest in this kind of setting, make sure to dedicate one-on-one time with that person and get to know them fully outside of the group, too. Alone time is sexy; make that person feel like they have your undivided attention.

- Events and nights out – Be bold, be brave, and if you can't bring yourself to make the first move, at least make it obvious to whoever you fancy that they're welcome to hit on you. Eye contact and body language are going to be your best friends in this kind of environment; it's going to be loud and so probably not somewhere you're going to have a lot of conversation. Just don't forget to grab their digits before the night is over, or if they end up in the Uber home with you, remember that sexual health is sexy, so don't be afraid to ask when they last got tested.

There is a myriad of different ways of flexing your dating muscles; you could meet someone in the workplace, through friends or on the bus home. And remember that within the spectrum there are a plethora of different types of relationships and sexualities to learn about and explore. Queerness is complex and you'll find that we're much more in tune with who we are dating and how we feel about dating than our straight fam. There are more and more of us who identify as polyamorous, have open relationships, are demisexual, asexual and the list goes on. I've always known for the most part that I'm monogamous – I only have romantic relationships with one person at a time – and so have most often pursued those who feel the same. What I've also made sure to do is be very honest about what I'm looking for.

Meet Jess and Heather...

I'm Jess Gardham, my pronouns are she/her and I identify as a lesbian.

And I'm Heather Grogan, also she/her and, I hate the sexuality question, but I identify as bisexual.

H: I feel like as soon as you say the word bisexual people just dismiss it and think you're saying it for attention, or make you feel like it's not valid even though it is, and that is what I am. Looking back, I think if I'd had gay friends when I was young or if there had been queer people in the media it might have clicked sooner for me. But it just never even entered my brain that it was a thing, that it was even possible.

J: I dated guys until I was in secondary school and then there was an incident where we were in the changing rooms getting ready for PE. A girl who I was good friends with stood in front of me in her bra just chatting to me and I felt my heart go really fast. I was like, 'Oh my god! I think I like girls.' But I never dared say anything. I kept it a secret until college where there were a few gay girls in my friendship group and I remember thinking they were so cool. They were so themselves, so confident and I thought, you know what? I can start to be a bit more open about it now.

H: In my early twenties I was engaged to a guy, had moved to Australia and back again before meeting Jess for the first time in the reception of the dental practice I took a job at. She worked there too and I remember thinking, 'Oh, she's really lovely.' Over time it was unspoken, this comfortable feeling between us. We'd known each other for a year before I got married and I asked Jess to sing at my wedding and the connection we had then was that we were best friends.

J: The change in our dynamic was gradual over the next four years. I remember small things like her walking past me and my head would just follow her down the corridor. She's got a beautiful walk. Then over time it started getting more flirty, to the point where people around us could see this kind of attraction that was just growing and growing, getting stronger and stronger. On a night out in Glasgow, things went up a level. Alcohol was involved and suddenly Heather took my hand and led me through the crowd and we didn't say a word to each other, but we knew what was gonna happen. We kissed, and it just cemented everything. People think everything's black or white when it comes to love and relationships, but it really isn't.

H: It was such a complicated time, but I told my husband and my family, and funnily enough most people knew that it was Jess. It's awful telling someone that you don't love them any more, but we were meant to be together. We were probably meant to meet way before and if we had I probably never would have got married in the first place.

J: I thought Heather's family was going to see me as a pred-ator. As this lesbian woman coming in, splitting up this beautiful, young heterosexual couple who are gonna have babies and a white picket fence life. Luckily, it was the complete opposite, and that's testament to the fact that we've both grown up in families that are all about the love for their child. They understand trials, tribulations and complications happen in life and both our families have been there to support us individually.

H: We've been together now for five years (known each other for ten) and I would say only this year I've really settled on how I identify. Being with Jess has opened me up to a whole new world of things I wasn't aware of and people that I wasn't aware of before. It took a while, but I think everyone has the potential to be a bit gay to be honest! It all depends on how open you are to it. We communicate really well, which is why I think we have the relationship we do. If one of us is in a bit of an assy mood or is on our period, we just seem to communicate really well. You have to make an effort to maintain your connection and I think people can forget that it's two sided. It shouldn't just be one of you that initiates closeness and intimacy all the time because that person will get sick of it. It has to be a two-way thing.

J: We've maintained our relationship because we know each other inside out. We've seen each other in other relationships, we've seen each other when we've been upset, when we're angry, at work, tired, annoyed. We have that friendship basis.

H: This is going to sound really sickening, but you hear some people who have been in a relationship for a long time say, 'It's not how it used to be.' But every time we have sex it's like it's the first time. I'll never get sick of Heather flicking her hair over her shoulder. It's so sexy!

Jess Gardham and Heather Grogan

Depending on where you're at in life, you might be open to meeting your life partner, looking for casual sex, dating a few different people at once and so on. All of those things are absolutely fine, as long as you tell the people who you're spending time with exactly where you're at. Being up front and honest gives people the chance to decide whether you're the right person for them to be investing time and energy into. It's also just real basic respect not to lead people on or to ghost them. Try to treat people how you want to be treated yourself, and if you're thinking, 'Helen, I can barely think about what I'd do on a first date with a girl, let alone having multiple on the go,' let's get first date ready as I give you a run-down of the best ways you can prepare yourself when meeting anyone new.

- Dress to impress – Wear something that you feel comfortable in, but don't be afraid to add a little sexy to the mix. Being overdressed is always better than looking scruffy, and if in doubt, call ahead and find out what the dress code is.

- Timeliness is hot af – Please don't be late, I beg you; it's my biggest ick.

- Out yourself – If you're feeling nervous, just tell the person that's how you feel. Chances are they'll double down on their efforts to help make you feel relaxed, and vulnerability is always hot.

- Have the manners of a saint – I hope you always do tbh, and yes, I'm British, but saying please and thank you and speaking to wait staff politely are just basic manners that make a great first impression.

- Listen, ask questions and then listen some more – Being interested in the other person and not talking about yourself the entire time makes the other person feel like you really care about what they have to say.

- Don't be afraid to get deep – Sure, the general stuff about where you grew up and how many siblings you've got is great, but what is that really telling you about someone? Don't be afraid to really connect.

In between all of the weird and wonderful experiences, I've had deep and meaningful long-term relationships, too. I have to say, bar one (we don't speak of the devil around here), I've had truly incredible girlfriends. I have so much love for every partner I've been with because of the integral parts they've each played in my life and my growth. You might be thinking, 'Isn't it weird to say that you have love for all of your exes?' Well, you might need to get used to it, because lesbians have this innate skill of continuing to love and cherish our ex-girlfriends long after relationships have ended. Queers in general oftentimes maintain close friendships with their exes throughout their lives. Maybe not all of them, and maybe not forever, but it happens a lot. And this is very much a queer thing. Just ask a straight pal if they're friends with all of their exes and they'll look at you in horror.

I don't know if it's because we're so emotionally intelligent, more in touch with our feelings, grateful to have had love, or what. But it's a real knack, and I personally have partaken in this behaviour throughout my life. I say partake because it's a choice that I don't think should be taken as lightly as some of us do. So much has to be right for remaining friends with an ex to really work. There have to be boundaries, time passed since the relationship ended and respect for the new space that you find each other in. Becoming friends with someone after you've been in a relationship with them can mean that you find it hard to let go of the person you once knew, which can have a negative impact on the both of you. The relationships I had in my early twenties were so personality building that I wanted to stay friends with my exes to maintain a feeling of safety in someone really 'knowing me'. These days, I think much more carefully about whether it's necessary to maintain a friendship with someone I've been in love with, because it's a real balancing act that impacts the way you move forward in your life. As lesbians or queer people, you'll encounter this in some way throughout your journey in the community; if it's not by you deciding to be friends with an ex, it'll be a girl you date, or a friendship group you're trying to navigate.

Something else universal to the lesbian population is that we tend to move very quickly in terms of our relationships. It's so universal that when I asked my followers on Instagram about their own experiences with what we call 'the urge to merge', I wasn't at all surprised by the results. I asked, 'What is the soonest you've told someone that you love them?' and seventy per cent of lesbians have said it within one month. That's quick, right?! Gals really be out there doing the most. I'm not calling it definitive research, but it's apparent across the lesbian community that we fall in love quickly and the urge to U-Haul (to move in with one another quickly) is real.

But why does this happen and what are the ramifications? There are a few different theories actually, one being that, as women, we're taught that our lives are defined by relationships. We're taught from a very young age that our purpose is to find a man and to get married and that's what defines our lives as being a success or not. But of course, we're gay! And so with potential low self-esteem and internalized lesphobia, plus the ingrained idea of having to have a relationship to live a happy/normal life, that may be why we find ourselves jumping into relationships quicker than you can say Ellen DeGeneres.

Another possible reason for it is that two women together are creating a hell of a lot of oxytocin, the love hormone. Women create more oxytocin than men do, so when you times that by two it could be a significant reason why we become attached far quicker, because love is, quite literally, in the air. Also, as queer people we have this inherent need to be understood, to be recognized in our queerness, and when you find someone who seemingly understands and who loves you deeply, that euphoria can catapult you into a honeymoon phase super quickly. There's no definitive answer I can give you, but ultimately it doesn't really matter.

There's no right or wrong timeframe for you to fall in love, to become committed to a person, to become girlfriends, get engaged or any of it, as we heard in Jess and Heather's love story. Whatever timeframe works for you is right for you. Of course the longer you date someone, the better you're going to know them and the deeper a connection you may have, but often gut instinct tells you everything you need to know, and you can't help how quickly you fall for someone. But amidst all of the intense emotions and wonderful feelings that you're feeling, it's worth just taking a breath and having a moment to yourself to do that thing that we're learning to do more and more of, and that's having a strong sense of self.

Throughout your relationships, to avoid losing yourself in that urge to merge, as much as we want to become a unit, a team with our partner, it's so important to maintain the personal identity that you've worked hard to forge. Of course when you love someone deeply and spend a lot of time together it's only natural that you might begin to mirror one another in certain ways, but a strong self-identity will help you to be a better partner in the long run. You'll be a much happier and more proficient version of you when you have autonomy over your own life and when you're achieving and thriving as your own person. Having a positive sense of self is imperative in navigating major life tasks, in achieving true intimacy with others and in finding your place in society. It's important that whilst, yes, it's wonderful to be truly, madly, deeply in love with someone, you're living a fulfilled life in your own way, in your own body, through your own experiences.

If you're feeling swept up by a relationship, if you're feeling like you're a little out of control or as though you're so heady it's hard to think straight, ask yourself or even journal your responses to these questions, to help bring yourself back down to earth:

- What are the things outside of my relationship that I love and enjoy?

  It could be hobbies, seeing friends and family, learning new skills or spending time with pets. Then ask yourself how long you spend doing these things on a weekly basis. You'll know if you need to make adjustments, and I want you to actively do so if necessary.

- Do I think about and act on what I want as much as I do my partner's needs?

   Again, your response will tell you if there are some things you need to change. Remember that a relationship should be fifty-fifty. Sometimes you'll need to pick up a little slack here and there, but for the most part, you should be treating each other as equals.

- How much time am I spending pursuing my goals and taking alone time?

   You should be able to spend time alone without feeling at a loss or even lonely. You are your own best friend, and whilst you might be more of a social person, you should still be able to take time to yourself and enjoy it. To be able to do things like self-reflect and self-care. You should also feel supported in the way of pursuing things that are important to you. Life is so short, make sure you don't miss out on pursuing those dreams before it's too late.

- Am I saying yes when I really mean no?

   As a serial people pleaser, it's sometimes easier just to go along with what the other person wants to do and for a while it feels good to be so amiable. But putting someone else's needs before your own will only lead to resentment down the line. Compromise is important in a relationship, but always putting the other person first will come at a cost.

- Am I being my authentic self?

   Are you being one hundred per cent you? Because only when you are will you be able to be truly happy, and don't you want to be happy? It's so much easier being you than living a life as someone or something else. Once you can accept and step into that vulnerability, it will let you reach a level of happiness and contentment in yourself like you've never known.

One of my relationships that had me swept off of my feet was with Chloe. She was a security manager. She was built, strong, had an accent, and was such an engaging person. Full of conversation, passionate in bed, a real people person, and it was enchanting getting to know her. I'd had some therapy by this point, had figured out some of my weak spots and had been working on them diligently. I fell in love with her and we were pretty solid from the get go. We were the kind of couple people were envious of, and after a year and a half of dating, I knew that wanted to marry her. I proposed on Christmas Day, which we spent celebrating with her family, and I was so excited to get it right this time.

We'd been together for two years when things started to unravel, and by unravel I mean that our sex lives came to an abrupt stand-still because we'd merged so hard that we were more friends than fiancées. Eyelash extensions came first, then lip filler, then dresses and heels to the point where she just didn't feel like the person who I'd met, and I don't know if you remember but at the beginning of this chapter, I told you what my type was. I was so happy that she was stepping more and more into her true identity through our relationship, but although our personalities hadn't necessarily changed, I couldn't force myself to fancy someone who no longer existed to me.

The merging of two people doesn't always end in heartbreak. That emotional openness you share with another queer person can result in hasty decisions, but it can also be really positive, too. As I write, I'm ten months into the best relationship of my life and we've U-Hauled to an extent. We live together most of the time at my girlfriend's place, but I also still rent a flat in London so that we have our own space should we need it. I also have full faith that at no time in the future will Becky be asking to borrow my lippy, which suits me perfectly. Importantly, we spend time alone, have nights out with our own pals, pursue life goals together as well as personal ones alone and champion each other being our true selves, always. She's playing the PlayStation as we speak, and I think it's time she has my full attention, so I'll leave you with this.

Dating is wonderful; it's a gift and privilege to be welcomed into someone else's life. So enjoy it, have fun, be respectful and test your boundaries. When you do find that person, or people, who you just can't get enough of, let yourself freefall and hold on tight for the ride. Just remember that for longevity, when you *feel* your best, you can *show up* as the best for your significant other. You should always be your biggest priority, and everything else will follow, promise.

Chapter 6

Once a Lesbian, Always a Lesbian?

et's talk for a second about sexuality and gender (as if that's not what we've been doing for the last five chapters), because there's a very real difference between the two and this is where a lot of people get confused. It's okay if that's you; we're educating ourselves always, so let's just take a moment to make sure we're all on the same page.

Sexuality is in reference to who we fancy, who we're attracted to: men, women, non-binary people, and so on. The official definition is:

> **sexuality**
> /sɛkʃʊˈaləti/
> *noun*
> I. A person's identity in relation to the gender or genders to which they are typically attracted; sexual orientation.
> 'people with proscribed sexualities'

Gender is how you identify and feel on the inside: male, female, floating somewhere in the gorgeous in between, etc. The proper definition is:

> **gender**
>
> /ˈdʒɛndə/
>
> *noun*
>
> 1. Either of the two sexes (male and female), especially when considered with reference to social and cultural differences rather than biological ones. The term is also used more broadly to denote a range of identities that do not correspond to established ideas of male and female.
> 'a condition that affects people of both genders'

In this book we're talking mostly about sexuality, and yes, the word lesbian is in the title, but I hope that by now you understand that everything I'm talking about is, and can be, experienced by anyone on the queer spectrum. Similarly with gender, I may refer to women more heavily in this book (it's about time lesbian women had something positive to stake claim over), but everything we're discussing is for my entire LGBTQ+ family, too. As I've said before, we may not all be on the same ship and heading in the same direction, but we're all out here on this rainbow-coloured ocean together and can relate to one another in a way that no one else can.

The reason that I wanted to start with the definitions of gender and sexuality is because when they're described as simply as possible, it's easy to imagine how and why these two things may not be as solid and cemented in our identities as we are taught to believe. Not for all of us, but these two things can so easily flow and change throughout our lifetimes depending on our situations, experiences, relationships and growth. Throughout our lives there is so much that changes and evolves – we move house, jobs, we trial different haircuts and try new hobbies – so why is it such an outlandish idea that who we fancy might change too?

I've always felt very female. Very attached to my femininity, I love all things that are attached to the feminine identity, like heels and make up and lacy lingerie. However, it's definitely the new-age female identity that I associate with. Growing up, I was constantly told I was too loud, too outspoken, too brash and too athletic; I wasn't a dainty girl who would do as she was told. I'm a boss bitch who speaks her mind, pays her own bills and has as much sex as she likes. I'm not oblivious to the 'masculine traits' that I have. I'm very tall, I command a conversation, I'm always the driver and never the passenger, but although I'm a new-age woman, I still very much identify as just that. My sexuality, on the other hand, has ebbed and flowed over the years and I've had, well, questions.

Because I'm a cis woman (a woman who identifies with the sex I was assigned at birth), I don't want to take up too much space in this book discussing gender. Hell, I'll advocate all day, but there are so many other incredible humans who talk about it in a much more interesting way than I do and with much more depth. Of course, you know your girl's linked some books and creators in the resources section for you. I feel like gender can be a really imprisoning part of society that stops humanity's freedom of expression. Man, woman, non-binary, it's just another beautiful facet of human nature that can evolve like anything else in life. Just because you're born with certain biological attributes doesn't determine how you feel on the inside, and it's how you *feel* that determines your gender, not how you pee. Once you've finished this book, I encourage you to pick up a book on gender, regardless of how you identify, and I encourage you to develop and open your mind to other people's points of view. Our trans and non-binary siblings are in an extremely vulnerable and scary place with gender politics right now; they need our love and support more than ever.

Around the time that I came out, I met Nikki, Essex's version of Shane from *The L Word*. Totally androgynous, with a strong jawline and who wore baggy jeans and a vest with no bra. I'd never seen anyone like them. We became close very quickly, and soon after we'd met they shared with me that they were intersex. Intersex is the term that a person may use when they have both male and female sex characteristics. These characteristics include genitalia, hormones, chromosomes and reproductive organs, and at the time, there was so little knowledge about those who are intersex and even today it is something without much wider education. Even Nikki themselves didn't have the language to describe their own body or their uniqueness, and looking back I know that their mental health suffered. They felt unsure about where they fit within society. It must have been incredibly confusing to grow up intersex in an era that hadn't evolved quick enough to even have the language for it. It's estimated that up to 1.7 per cent of the population has an intersex trait and that approximately 0.5 per cent of people have clinically identifiable sexual or reproductive variations. They're the 'I' in the LGBTQIA+ acronym and so, of course, I've listed some creators in the directory for you to go follow, learn from and support.

I talk about this experience because Nikki didn't identify as male or female, and remember we're basing this on gender, the way they identified, not referring to their biological physicality. You may also have noticed the use of they/them pronouns as I was talking about them. They just felt like they floated around in the middle. However, we didn't have the non-binary label back then and we certainly didn't have the pronoun awareness that we do today, and so it wasn't an easy thing for them to explain or to fully grasp themselves. They used she/her pronouns when I knew them, but as we're no longer in contact I'm using they/them pronouns as things may well be different nowadays. I discussed with the Famalam, over on InstaStories, how I should refer to them in the book, and we all agreed that they/them would be best so as not to assume or offend. I bring all of this up to say that those who are intersex can identify as any gender or sexuality that they choose because, remember, gender isn't determined by biological features. In this instance Nikki was non-binary, queer and intersex. They had a lot going on at a time when we really didn't have the language to discuss their nuances at capacity. Thankfully a lot has changed since then and our vocabularies have expanded to make room for our more diverse and advanced understanding of sexuality and gender. I didn't realize then that I was in a queer situationship, because we didn't know that's what it was back in 2008. But I was attracted to Nikki for who they were and the connection we had and so technically, and I'm about to potentially derail this entire book in one sentence, but technically, if we were to look at labels in black and white, I'm not a lesbian. I'm actually pansexual.

pansexual

/pan'sɛkʃʊəl/

adjective

1. Not limited in sexual choice with regard to biological sex, gender or gender identity.

Essentially, pansexual means that your attraction to someone isn't determined by their gender, but by who they are as a person. Now I can fancy pretty much anyone other than straight men (sorry guys, it's you, not me!). I'm attracted to those whose sexuality falls on the queer spectrum in some way, but in terms of gender, I've been known to dabble! And so yes, technically, pansexual would best describe my sexuality. However, I don't believe that anything is truly black and white when it comes to sexuality or gender, and I identify as a lesbian, through and through. I love women, I particularly love lesbians, and I know to my core that that's who I am. Even if I am attracted to those who identify outside of the female gender, my overriding sense of self is the lesbian inside me. Now, those who fall under the lesbian label are not all going to think and feel and experience things exactly the same way. Humans all have their variations, and that's true of any group or community too. It's what makes life so interesting, right? So if I'm a lesbian who has pansexual qualities, what does that then make me?

Thank god for the idea of sexual fluidity! Sexual fluidity is the term for the grey areas of the label that you identify with that don't quite match the description. For example, say for the most part you're attracted to women, but you've had a few relationships with men. You might not now identify as bisexual, but you may consider yourself somewhat fluid since you're not *exclusively* attracted to women. And that can be said with all of the genders and sexuality identities. This is where the term sexually fluid might be used, as it helps us to get around those black-and-white depictions of sexual orientation and is a wonderful way of being able to describe our grey area thoughts and feels.

Meet Cambell...

I'm Cambell Kenneford, my pronouns are she/her, and with my sexuality, I don't put a label on it. It's not that I don't like the word lesbian, but for me I've never identified as one. I also don't like the word pansexual, like pansexual just sounds so unsexy. I'm too sexy for pansexual.

I always felt different from a really young age. I was born 'technically' male, but I never felt that was who I was inside. I would always play with Barbies, or I'd have towels on my head pretending I was the Little Mermaid. I would cry to my mum asking, 'Why I aren't I a girl like my friends?' So it was from a really young age when I knew I was different from other boys. As time went on, I wore make up, I started growing my hair and started painting my nails. Then when I was fifteen, I transitioned officially. My pronouns changed. I told everyone this was what I was gonna do, and absolutely no one was shocked.

My mum has always been completely supportive. She'd take me to my hormone appointments, she'd come with me to have my surgery, she's been right there for me through everything. A lot of parents of trans people say they feel like they lost a son and gained a daughter, but my mum says she never felt that way. Having an unsupportive parent could've changed things so drastically for me, but because she was always so open with me being who I am, I just felt like I could always express myself and so she's been completely pivotal in who I am today.

Because I was so obsessed with my gender, getting my surgery, getting hormones, I didn't really have time to think about my sexuality. I think one of the biggest misconceptions is that sexuality and gender are the same thing. It wasn't something I thought about for a long time because I wasn't happy within myself and the way that I looked. As time went on, I forced myself into a relationship with a man because I felt that if I was with a man then it would make me feel more feminine. But upon reflection, I'm a woman and I don't need validation from a man to make me feel like a woman.

When I started hormones, my feelings started to change, and I realized, 'You know what, maybe I am attracted to women.' I was scared to tell people because it's kind of like coming out all over again, and I didn't know how well I'd be received in the lesbian community and that was something that really, really scared me.

Now it just doesn't faze me or affect me. I mean, people are always gonna have opinions but it's up to you how you deal with them. I always felt that being with a girl would make me feel more masculine for some reason, because I'd be comparing myself to her. Like for example, she has a period and I don't, and don't get me wrong, it did take me a long time to get over that, and that was something I really struggled with at the start of my current relationship, because I was used to being with a man and it was a very different situation, and then going out with a girl, it really fucked with my mind a bit, my dysphoria. But I've worked through that, and my girlfriend of three years has taught me so much about myself and has helped me to discover so much of my own womanhood that I didn't realize I didn't have before. I could just go on for days about how this relationship has changed my life. I just feel so happy, and this is where I'm meant to be right now.

Cambell Kenneford

Over the course of your life you might experience a change in who you're attracted to, the label you use to describe your sexuality and who you fancy and want to share intimacy with. On the flipside, you might have flown from the womb as lesbian as they come and that's how you'll remain until the day that you die. You might be reading this book, aged forty, and still not know what label you fall under, or have come out as non-binary and so how you label your sexuality is still in question. We go deep diving into labels in the next chapter, but ultimately your sexuality does not define who you are. It doesn't define if you're a good or bad person, how worthy of love and respect you are or how happy and fulfilled your life can be. Labels simply act as a guide to help understand how you feel. Useful yes, but not #bible.

There's a lot of stigma around those who experience sexual fluidity, or who change their label or identity, and they are often hugely undermined, seen to be following trends and are not taken seriously because the greater world wants them to pick a side or a team and stay in that lane forever because it's easier to understand and categorize each other that way. Consciously or unconsciously, another stigma around sexual fluidity or a change in orientation is that you might be sexually promiscuous or nonmonogamous, and no one can sympathize with those feelings and experiences better than our bisexual peers. Even from within the community we need to put an end to the small-minded, ignorant and damaging stigma surrounding sexual fluidity of any kind. It can cause a mental health symptom known as minority stress, which you'd think, as a minority group ourselves, we'd all be a little more attuned to. To be further stigmatized within a minority group can have serious implications, and quite frankly, I want to see the wider community do better huns.

Our mental health is already at a higher risk than that of the hetero community, and so being there for one another is the very least that we can do. So long as you're not harming yourself or other humans, whatever you feel about your sexuality or gender, if it changes and you want to acknowledge those changes, that's okay. Humans are so wonderfully complex; you're bound to have varying feelings throughout your life. We're curious beings and it's perfectly normal to explore those. I'm a grown-ass queer woman and throughout my lifetime so far I've been straight, lesbian, pansexual, monogamous, polyamorous, demisexual and vegan. Who cares? So long as you're following your own path and being true to you, it doesn't bloody matter.

It was after a rather long stint of very bad dates that I discovered polyamory. After dating what felt like hundreds of women, tall, short, fat, thin, ambitious, pensive, outlandish and brooding, I got to the point where I thought I should broaden my horizons and not put all of my eggs into one lesbian basket. Maybe I hadn't found 'the one' because I actually need two or three humans to fulfil different desires and sides of myself. I even went on a podcast and broadcast these ideas out loud (I never do things by halves) and pursued polyamory with a vengeance. After dating multiple humans at the same time for around six months, I realized that I just don't have the emotional capacity, or frankly, the stamina, to date multiple people at once. Being able to emotionally freefall with more than one person was just too much for my brain and heart to comprehend. I also couldn't get my head around the idea of sharing, which is I think most people's roadblock when exploring nonmonogamy. Jealousy is a tricky thing to navigate! But deep down, I want to be somebody's some*one*; that's just the kind of gal I am. And so I concluded that I am a monogamous human after all.

Around the same time as my flirtation with polyamory, I had my first experience of dating someone who openly identified as non-binary, which is when I first discovered the pansexual label. I remember feeling disappointed to discover that maybe I wasn't a lesbian after all, and I went through a period of experiencing real guilt around my lesbian identity that I had advocated for my whole life, had lost things for and had carved my life around. I actually felt like I'd lost my identity to an extent because something about the pansexual label just didn't feel right, although with some of my experiences it was maybe a more accurate depiction. I was also concerned that if I openly identified as lesbian, and people saw me dating someone who is non-binary, they'd judge me or call me out for it, and I really did some deep soul searching trying to figure this out.

It's scientifically proven that sexuality is on a spectrum, so of course there are going to be blurred lines and grey areas. Research supports both the idea that broad terms or labels can be misleading for some people and the idea that people often have sexual orientation *ranges*. And so yes, you may yourself moving about the spectrum over the course of your lifetime as you grow and evolve and experience new things, and it's important that you don't put pressure on yourself if that happens. We're humans, complicated mazes of creatures, and so of course there will be lots of us who don't quite fit one or the other, and especially if your sexuality is more fluid, then you might just span all the way across it, rainbow style.

What I came to realize was that fancying someone who identifies as non-binary doesn't make me any less of a lesbian. And that if it would make me uncomfortable giving up my lesbian identity, then I didn't have to! This is where labels really are taken with a pinch of salt. Yes, everyone has an underlying orientation, mine being lesbian, for example. Yet there's room for things to expand a little, based on your experiences and current situation, and for me that was to include a select few non-binary humans that I just so happen to have had a connection with throughout my life. I'm open to the idea that my lesbian identity has an edge of fluidity to it, and I know that I'm not alone in that. The changes in how you experience romantic and sexual attraction are totally valid and are, you know I hate to use the word, normal.

Meet Kelsey and Luke...

I'm Kelsey Pearson, she/her and I identify as pansexual.

And I'm Luke Pearson, he/him and I'm straight.

K: Luke and I met on Instagram in 2015. He was sharing online workout programmes, and I was his second client ever. Truth be told, I didn't care about his workout plan, I just wanted to talk to him. At the time, Luke still presented as the gender he was assigned at birth, and I wouldn't meet the *actual* Luke for another five and a half years. After getting married in 2019, Luke came out as trans in 2021, and we've been on the journey of a lifetime together, finding his identity and our identity as a couple.

L: Since I was a kid, I couldn't really relate to the girls my age. I remember feeling like I was the boy on my softball teams and was interested in gender stereotypical hobbies, toys and activities for boys. I think this made my parents think I was gay from a young age and a tomboy, instead of having a conversation about gender identity with me. The world saw me as a girl and I had to find a way to get in line and fit those expectations. So I shoved those gender struggles down deep and tried to forget them. I felt immense envy when seeing a guy I knew in middle school share his transition on Instagram. Every cell in my body was trying to get my attention, but I didn't voice those feelings for years, I just kept watching him, feeling that jealousy, wishing that was me. Once I was ready to accept my truth and I voiced these feelings out loud, I felt this wave of relief, like a pressure valve had been released. I could finally start listening to myself again, uncovering those years of gender identity questions and feelings that I had buried for so long, and really get to know myself.

K: Before Luke came out as trans, he came out as non-binary. I opened the door a few times, asking if he thought he might be trans and he'd say no, but I could see through his eyes that his mind was at work. One day I was at the bookstore, and I came across a book written by a trans guy (*Trans Mission: My Quest to a Beard* by Alex Bertie) and I read the first page – a letter to his dad. I felt like I was reading a letter Luke wrote, and I knew I needed to get the book for him. That night, he read the whole book in one sitting and asked me to read it, too. Luke came out to me in our parking garage, sitting in our car chatting a few days later, and he looked at me with tears in his eyes and said, 'I'm a boy.' I didn't have to do much work to accommodate the change. I honestly didn't think about myself at all. I knew then, like I know now, that Luke is my person. I don't care how he identifies; I just care that he's happy. We simply jumped into this journey together, and we've figured it out along the way.

L: This feels like a brand-new life and I'm so grateful to have an amazingly supportive and loving wife who made me feel safe to open up to her, and explore what this journey would mean to me. It means everything.

K: It was easy to fall into the lesbian identity. All of our friends were lesbians, we were growing a predominantly lesbian following on social media, etc. But if asked directly, I'd say I was bisexual. When Luke came out as trans, it reminded me how important it is for me to also be true to myself. I identify as pansexual now (though bisexual would also be valid) as I just feel that pansexual relates more to how I feel. I have no preference on gender. I fell in love with Luke for his heart, and his personality and his humour. He now identifies as straight, but we are a queer couple.

K: We were both a bit shocked by some of the reactions we received when Luke came out. Whilst the majority of people who follow us online were extremely supportive, a handful were not. A shocking number of lesbians felt they'd 'lost another lesbian', which is a sad take on someone finding their true identity. Luke was never a lesbian, even if he presented as one. For me, I received comments insinuating I 'appropriated lesbian culture'. We as humans are constantly learning

about ourselves, and with new knowledge comes new understanding. Like our interests, sexuality can change. Hell, there
was a time I thought I was straight until I realized I wasn't.

I am holding tight to my queerness. Since we now appear
as a heterosexual couple, it is important to me that I maintain
my identity as a pansexual woman. Labelling my identity is
how I finally found my own acceptance. It's how I found
community. I hope that when people see us, they see two
people who unconditionally love each other. But we are queer.
We're definitely queer.

Kelsey Pearson and Luke Pearson

It can be confusing to have fluctuations in your sexuality, especially when it can take a hot minute just stepping into your
queerness to begin with. It's never easy navigating changes
when perhaps you've just got settled or have accepted who
you are. For some of us, you may experience more life-alter-
ing changes in your sexuality, like Luke, realizing your gender
doesn't match that of the lesbian orientation any longer and
so whole new terms and labels are needed. Regardless of
your experience, they're all exciting and positive changes that
are leading you to being your most authentic self, which, as
confusing as things can feel sometimes, is the most important
thing. And similarly, if nothing changes with regards to your
sexuality on your journey through life, that's totally normal
for you too, because we're each on our own path.

For some of us, we might not even realize that we're gay
until much later in life, or we've always known and have
been repressing it until we can hold it in no longer. It's not
always in our late teens or twenties that we come flouncing
out of the closet, and coming out later in life comes with its

own unique challenges, but no doubt has *huge* benefits, too. Having financial independence and a more solid sense of self as we get older might lead those who have pushed their sexuality to one side for family life or to simply abide by societal norms to say, 'No more!' The average age for people to come out is getting younger, but studies have indicated that there are up to four million LGBTQ+ adults over the age of sixty in the US.[1] I think that's in part due to the influx of acceptance and representation surrounding the community, I mean, just look at the likes of Cynthia Nixon, Mary Portas and Sarah Paulson. Women who have repressed feelings about their sexuality have reached a point where they no longer want to settle for an unfulfilled life, and I don't blame them!

Of course there are no doubt going to be challenges if you do come out later on in life and there's lots to consider, particularly if you have children. But at what cost and to whose benefit would it be for you to live your one very short life forcing yourself to be someone you're not? Any kind of significant change in yourself will always require a huge level of self-care and reflection, and so if you're joining the community in this type of scenario, be kind to yourself first and foremost, take time and space to adjust and calibrate your thoughts and then buckle up for a whole heap of fun as you step into who you were born to be. Coming out in your forties, fifties or even sixties plus might have people looking at you like you've lost the plot, but, can I be frank with you? Fuck 'em. It's your life, grab it by the (metaphorical) balls and do what feels right to you because before you know it, it'll all be over. Who wouldn't want to live life in rainbow colour anyway?

Sexual fluidity has its own challenges outside of simply coming out; it can make you feel 'othered' all over again, guilty, confused and a whole host of other things. On the other hand, it can feel incredibly empowering or freeing to have a better fit for how you feel. No matter what you're experiencing in relation to your sexuality, there's no need to go through it alone. Questioning your sexuality, even when you're already out, is a perfectly healthy activity. Talking about it with other people, as you know, can help you work through it more effectively and start to feel more settled in your thoughts. Don't feel pressured to settle on a label either. In the next chapter we're going to discuss whether we even need labels at all. There are plenty of people in the community who don't need, or even want, a label.

As you'll read throughout this book from the many thriving queers who are here to inspire you, when you're happy in yourself, it doesn't bloody matter what label you've got. You'll come to realize that life isn't about 'what' you are, it's about 'how' you're living it to the max!

Chapter 7

Labels, Shmabels... Do We Need Them?

lesbian

/ˈlɛzbɪən/

noun

1. A woman who is sexually attracted to other women; a gay woman.

The main issue I faced when I approached publishers with my idea for *Live, Laugh, Lesbian* was the title. Their feedback was that using a title with the word lesbian was too 'niche' and that using the word queer instead would be much more 'inclusive' and open me up to a wider audience. But I'm not queer. And a lot of people out there aren't just queer either. I hope I've made it clear by now that you can be inclusive of the entire community and yet still champion the lesbians of the world at the same time. There's no need to erase a label in the process of doing that, and yet that's what's happening these days. And so the title of this book was reason enough for publishers to dismiss me, and I say 'dismiss *me*' purposefully, because that's exactly what they did. They didn't say no to the book, they said no to lesbians. They said no to my identity. Yet, head online and you'll find that the hashtag lesbian has been used 19.7 million times on Instagram (at the time of going to print) and has 61.6 *billion* views on TikTok. But they want me to have a wider audience? I call systemic homophobia, Famalam. I call lesbian erasure.

As we've already talked about, the word lesbian has been stripped away from us. It's been hijacked by groups of people who have no right or claim over the word and it's tarnished an entire community of people. I've championed the word lesbian my whole life, and if you're reading this and are (understandably) one of the lesbians who uses gay or queer only because of the negative connotations, I urge you to re-think. It's your sexuality, it's your identity and your choice, one hundred per cent. But don't let what other people think of the word lesbian dictate your right to use it. I know I can sound a little pushy, but don't mistake my enthusiasm for judgement. I merely mean to remind you that you have the right to decide for yourself on which terms you use. As your lesbian big sister, I'm here to simply open your mind to why you feel the way you do about the lesbian label and to remind you that it's something to be said proudly, if that's what you associate with.

After all, it's lesbians who protested on the streets of Manchester in one of the first Section 28 repeal marches here in the UK; it's lesbians who began the fight for marriage equality and who fought for equal IVF (in vitro fertilization) treatment for queer families. And it was lesbians who first began marching for our gay brothers during the HIV pandemic of the eighties in the US. We're a true force to be reckoned with! Our lesbian ancestors fought so painstakingly hard for our rights for equality and I can't help but feel that the least we can do is say the word with pride. Lesbians have forged the development of acceptance for the LGBTQ+ community throughout history and we're doing them a disservice by disassociating from the word because of how the world has weaponized it, rather than claiming it back to use as we wish.

I know it's easy for me to say. I'm white, blonde, femme presenting and live in London, which is one of the most LGBTQ+ friendly cities in the word. And I'm here banging on about how you should be out, be proud and not let our ancestors down. I wouldn't blame you for eye rolling at this point, but please just get to the end of the chapter at least before throwing this book in the bin. Because for all my banging on about reclamation, I'm not blind to the fact that times are changing and that it's not just fear of the word that makes people sidestep it. And whilst yes, there are some lesbians who won't use the word because of the way it sounds and the connotations that come with it, I think another reason more and more people are choosing queer or gay rather than lesbian runs much deeper than that, both culturally and politically.

Nowadays, particularly with the help of social media, queer communities and friendship groups tend to comprise a more diverse group of people than ever before. Historically, even during my late teens, we all kind of stuck to our letters under the acronym and it's only over the past few years that the lines are beginning to blur and we're breaking down the boundaries between us (I live for this, btw). More and more, friendship groups comprise a much more diverse LGBTQ+ tribe. Cisgender and transgender women, transgender men and transmasculine people and those who identify as non-binary or genderqueer are all coming together and bonding like never before. In that sense, 'lesbian' feels kinda outdated when you're surrounded by those who don't solely identify as women. Gen Z are leaning hard into this and I can see why, as more and more young people are exploring their gender and sexuality, and are shunning labels altogether or are identifying new, more accurate ones. The word lesbian can feel, well, old! And it wouldn't be the first time in history that we moved away from a label entirely.

There have been many words to describe different sexualities since language was created, and these words, much like the newer labels of today, have come into popularity only to be forgotten or sidestepped for better and more accurate depictions over the years. 'Tribade' is an old word for lesbian women and one that I only learned about whilst researching the use of labels for this book. It comes from the Greek word 'tribas', women who have sex with women, and in turn came from an older Greek word that meant 'to rub' (I'm obsessed!). According to literature, this was the most common word for lesbians in the seventeenth and eighteenth centuries and I'm kind of here for it! Then we have the word 'invert', which was used in the late nineteenth and twentieth centuries to refer to gay men and women because of gender-inversion theories. Many gay and lesbian activists at that time described homosexuality as a form of inversion too, to refer to the fact that they felt it was an innate part of them and beyond their control. Nowadays, those words are long gone and yet as we know, language, labels and expressions are evolving rapidly to help better depict the more intricate ways in which we're able to identify ourselves.

Another word we've outgrown that I don't think *sounds*

great, but had good intentions, is homophile. After World War II, there was another big wave of queer activism (see, we've been around for centuries and centuries) and a lot of this activism focused on presenting LGBTQ+ people as 're-spectable' in an attempt to gain widespread acceptance. The word homosexual, they felt, wasn't doing them any favours. The '-phile' comes from the Greek word for love, so using homophile stressed love instead of sex, which is kind of bang on the nose to be honest. But then, in the 1960s and 1970s, LGBTQ+ people started using the words gay and lesbian, and those have been the popularist phrases ever since. The reason I'm giving you a history lesson on labels is because, I get it, 'lesbian' might be becoming a thing of the past, and that's okay if there are better labels, more fitting labels, that suit how you feel on the inside. But make it your *choice* to use a different label, not your only option in a world that makes you feel bad for it.

Meet Jade...

My name is Jade Laurice, my pro-nouns are she/her. I would say my sexuality is always different when talking to different people. For me, I don't like to label myself too much, but I guess online and in certain set-tings I say I'm bisexual, but I'm sex-ually fluid. I feel like sexuality can change at any point of your life, so I don't like to put myself in too much of a box.

Being dual heritage, I'm already a minority. I grew up in a very white town and there were no Black people in my family that I was around, so I was always the brown girl in school, in my family, in the town. Then I started getting these feelings towards women, it was like a double whammy for me. I think that's why I didn't come out as early as I wanted to. I was already dealing with my identity as a brown person, as a person of colour.

I've always been attracted to people that are unique, people that stand out, people that have a quirky look about them and like to express themselves through their aesthetic, and back home it's not really like that. My sexuality didn't really hit me until I broadened my horizons, moved to London, and really started seeing what I liked. I felt like I'd just found myself because your sexuality is a big part of your identity, but it's not your full identity. It's feeling like, 'Oh my god, this is where I actually belong. This is what I'm meant to be doing, and *who* I'm meant to be doing.'

The past five years have been such a beautiful awakening, not just for my queerness but for my Blackness as well. It's been amazing and London was the reason for that, I guess. I wouldn't have been happy had I stayed in my hometown. My Blackness is a part of me, my queerness is a part of me, and not being able to have that back home was just so hard. I was so timid and quiet, I didn't really have many friends. So to have this life now where I'm so open on social media, I've got a bunch of friends, I'm very open with every part of me, is the whole 360. It's amazing to be in this city of possibilities.

I think dating women is harder (than dating men) because it makes me become more vulnerable. It makes me open up more, and I never really did that when I was dating men in the past. Unfortunately, a lot of men aren't open with their sensitivity or with their feelings, and in a way, I didn't realize it was making me not express mine as much. Being with women forced me to tell people how I'm feeling, and express myself a little bit more. It definitely made me more vulnerable, which was harder, but in the long run it's been a good thing. I also realize as well that if I ever date a man again, I would just choose someone who is more sensitive and open with his feelings. It was just the men that I dated before. Even saying this, I think we're really lucky that we're in this generation and live in the UK where we're able to safely express ourselves and be open with our sexuality, because it's not as easy for a lot of people around the world.

Because I date both genders, it's not always been easy to know what I want, who I want or what I want to end up dating. And I think once I loosened that pressure off myself and said to myself, 'Let it happen. If you end up with a man, you end up with a man. If you end up with a woman, you end up with a woman,' it felt easy. Until then I was fighting with my own mind. Letting go is how I have a really amazing relationship with myself now.

Jade Laurice

I've hosted a lesbian festival in the UK for the last nine years called L Fest. Catchy, right? And the festival is a family of a thousand women who gather every year to celebrate their love, connection and kinship over many alcoholic beverages and banging music artists. The festival has an average age of fifty to sixty, and the reason I'm bringing this up is because A) these women and queer people know how to party (trust me, older lesbians should not be slept on). And B) they grew up in a time where being out and proud wasn't as accepted, if it was accepted at all, and they could barely be out, let alone let their inner lesbians loose. Festivals like L Fest, and simply the word lesbian, are so important to them. To that era of queer women, the word represents the victory of overcoming a life spent either in the closet or fighting just to be alive. The word lesbian means something different to each of us. Remember what I've said before. Same sea, different ships.

All around it feels like there's a generational divide that's not super helpful in keeping the lesbian label alive. The stereotype is that elder lesbians are outdated on gender politics with the rise in affiliation with TERFs, or that they don't understand or aren't up to date with queer references in the media and online, and so I get it. What twenty-year-old wants to associate with that? Add to that the fact that more and more young people are exploring relationships with people who might not identify as a woman, who are non-binary or gender fluid and so the lesbian label feels too restrictive for their experiences. Even when two identifying women are in a relationship, there is oftentimes a masc/femme dynamic in terms of aesthetic, and so queer works better because lesbian implies a kind of likeness that isn't reflected in the outlook of the relationship. See, there are so many reasons the word is being rebuffed beyond the fact that it sounds 'icky'. And I won't lie, the word gay has been known to roll off of my tongue too, from time to time.

Ultimately, the L comes first, and even if I didn't personally identify as a lesbian, I want every letter in the acronym to have its place without shame and without stigma. Ultimately, we're a minority, growing by the day, yes, but if we don't stick up for one another, if we don't advocate for using labels freely for each other, who will? Queer terminology is diversifying thick and fast and is showing no signs of slowing down anytime soon. So I think it's important that we respect and uphold 'past' values whilst pushing forward and identifying new ones.

It's not just the lesbian label that comes with stigma; each letter of the acronym comes with its own baggage, associations, stereotypes and preconceptions. If you're bisexual you're greedy, polyamorous, a slut. And phew, if you're non-binary you're an attention seeking snowflake acting 'woke' for likes. It's a judgemental world out there, and judgement will always exist. But those elder lesbians who we may not feel akin to because they don't know who JoJo Siwa is spent a lot of their lives standing and fighting against prejudice, which allows us to get married, have babies and call ourselves lesbian if we choose to.

What I *do* think is that the more labels there are, the less pressure there is around choosing which one suits you best. With an abundance of information there's more freedom to pick and choose without the pressure to stick with one for life. The more and more it's talked about and understood in a way that isn't just black and white, making light of labels encourages us to be more playful with them. I think you'd be naive to think that the labels we have are nuanced enough to reflect all of our complexities as queer people. We've already talked about how they can change and evolve during your lifetime, and the importance of them to us individually may do the same. Learning about each one is the least that we can do to educate ourselves about other people and their experiences, but it doesn't mean you need to use them at all. We'll talk about that in a moment, but shall we do a quick run-down of some different labels you may come across and what they mean? Educated queers are the best queers, so let's go:

- **Lesbian** – A woman who is sexually and/or emotionally attracted to other women.

- **Gay** – Someone who is attracted to those of their same gender. It's most well known to describe men who are attracted to men.

- **Bisexual** – Someone who is sexually and/or emotionally attracted to more than one gender. Most typically, men and women.

- **Pansexual/omnisexual** – Individuals who are sexually and/or emotionally attracted to all genders and sexes including men, women, non-binary, trans and anyone in between.

- **Transgender** – Any person who has a gender identity that is different from the gender that they were assigned at birth.

- **Queer** – An umbrella term referring to anyone who is not straight and not cisgender. (Cisgender people are people whose gender identity and expression match the sex they were assigned at birth.)

- **Questioning** – Someone who isn't sure how they identify. Someone can be questioning their sexual orientation and/or their gender identity.

- **Intersex** – People who naturally have biological traits, such as hormonal levels or genitalia, that don't match what is typically identified as male or female. Being intersex is not linked to sexual orientation or gender identity.

- **Asexual** – Often referred to as 'ace', this is an umbrella term used for individuals who do not experience, or experience a low level of, sexual desire. People of different sexual orientations and gender identities can be asexual.

- **Ally** – People who identify as cisgender and straight and believe in social and legal equality for LGBTQ+ people.

- **Agender** – Those who don't identify as any gender at all.

- **Demisexual** – Someone who requires an emotional bond to form a sexual attraction with another human. People of different sexual orientations and gender identities can be demisexual.

- **Gender fluid** – Describes one's gender identity as being on a spectrum and not fixed to one specific gender.

- **Non-binary/genderqueer** – Those who don't conform to binary gender identities.

- **Polyamorous** – Those who are open to multiple consensual romantic or sexual relationships at one time.

- **Sapiosexual** – A person who is attracted to intelligence, regardless of a person's gender identity. People of different sexual orientations and gender identities can be sapiosexual.

- **Two-spirit** – A term used by Native Americans to describe a third gender, sometimes included as 2S in the main acronym as LGBTQIA2S+.

This list isn't exhaustive and is evolving, growing and diversifying all of the time. I know I've gone hard about the importance of not letting the lesbian label slip into obscurity, but another truth about why some of us are no longer adopting the term is simply because we don't care about labels altogether. Yes, they may help us to find the people who we want to connect with, which we know is important, but as you'll hear from some of the other voices throughout this book, labels don't always matter when you're happy just being you! We have a biological need to connect with others and feel 'a part' of something, and sometimes just knowing you're part of the community is enough.

Meet Abi...

I'm Abi, my pronouns are she/her and I identify as bisexual.

As a bi woman in my forties, separated from my husband and with almost two decades having passed since I last dated women, I was nervous to say the least. How the world had changed in that time and nowhere was this more apparent than on the dating apps and at queer club nights, where I mostly felt like a clueless teenager again. But this time with social media, a whole new queer vocabulary and a seemingly constant requirement to define myself. I knew butch and femme – neither of which felt like they fit me – but out of all the subcategories was there any way to fit?

Was I a tomboy femme? My gender expression tends to change from one day to another...sometimes super 'girly', other days wanting to reject the restrictions and expectations of being female, of being a mother, of the male gaze that I grew up with. And was I still bi if I knew I only wanted to date women? And that's before we even start talking sex and get into the question of top, bottom or switch (yep, I had to google). Confusing!

Growing up under Section 28, with virtually no resources

or role models, had meant I had always just had to define myself by myself, just tuning in to the specific dynamic of whatever relationship I was in and my partner's needs and desires. Talking to my girlfriend the other day I realized how much discarding certain labels benefited us both. How it liberated us from all the expectations that went with being a certain 'type' of queer woman and the need to fulfil a role or behave in a certain way.

So some labels felt disposable to me, but others required more thought, because I want to be loud and vocal about my sexuality for the sake of representation and in the hope of helping others in our community. I think labels can be instructive in helping us to recognize how our identities change over time and it's wonderful to feel at liberty to change one's label and not feel wedded to them or to have to justify or 'prove' them. I see and admire the way labels empower others.

These days people ask me if I'm a lesbian now that I'm in a long-term relationship with a woman – others just assume that I am, sigh – and whilst I love and admire my lesbian friends, I won't ever be one! Because that's just not my life experience. For me a crucial part of the process of making peace with my younger self was to do with embodying an identity that holds my past selves in it too and honours the wonderful previous relationships that I have had.

If I was a baby gay now I would likely gravitate to pan as a label for various reasons. However for me there is a politics to this too, and I feel an allegiance with the word bisexual as the first anchor I found when I was figuring out who I was in the nineties. I suppose it is an honouring of my roots in some ways. And it feels important to continue to advocate for our visibility. Similarly it's been interesting to see lesbian friends lean more into the word lesbian in recent years; it feels like there has been a reclaiming of this identity in a really positive and inclusive way.

We all approach and choose labels with different considerations in mind. In my view the main thing is to respect one another and validate each other, and also acknowledge that for some people labelling of their sexuality and gender is a longer process than for others: we all have our own timeframe.

Personally, I see and admire the way labels empower others, but ultimately my own romantic and sexual empowerment comes from the expansive and endless possibilities of just being me.

Abi Fellows

Labels can be harmful when they're forced on someone who doesn't want them, particularly in our youth when there's a lot of group pressure to say who and what you are and to stick to it. Particularly if you look or act a certain way, our world uses labels as a mental shortcut as to how we describe or define someone, and so you're then treated as per that mental shortcut that people associate you with. This doesn't always come with positive outcomes. We see it now in celebrity culture when a star's sexuality is ambiguous, or they haven't outrightly stated how they identify yet, and the whole world seems almost angry at them for not labelling themselves one way or another. Despite the increase in social acceptance for LGBTQ+ people around the world, coming out is still scary and hard for anyone at any age, regardless of whether you're famous or not, and this bullying behaviour via the media for people to out themselves is leading to a rejection of labels in defiance of this. Just look at Amy Schumer, deflecting any label and stating that she'd found her very own princess. A statement she should never have been forced to make, but very cleverly done on her part. Being labelled by other people, even if it fits, takes away your right to say for yourself how you identify, and no one should be forced to come out before they want to.

In a generation that's more fluid and questioning than ever, one in five young people worldwide identify as something other than straight, and one in ten American high-schoolers identify as gender diverse.[2] Those are incredible figures! I want to stress that these statistics don't pertain to 'new' thoughts and feelings by young people globally; gender diversity isn't new. We just so happen to live in a time where it's safe to explore our feelings, we have the language and support network to break it down and are bold enough to be who we really are. None of this is new, just the ability to express ourselves fully is.

Labels don't always make things better; it can be stressful to have to choose a label or identify a certain way when you need more time to figure things out. Sometimes they can hold us back when we put our own stigmas and limitations on how we should act, think and feel. But ultimately, only you get to say who you are, how you identify or if you want a label or not. It's totally up to you. You deserve autonomy over your identity. It's your basic human right, and don't let anyone tell you otherwise, including me.

Personally, I am so proud to call myself a lesbian (shock!) whilst standing firmly at the front of the acronym and empowering others to do the same. And in fact, you'll find out in the next chapter that there are some experiences (of the naked variety) that mean I colour outside of the lesbian labelled box, on occasion. My chosen label doesn't define me; it actually feels like more of a super power that I get to live in this judgement-free body every day, where all I want for us all is to love ourselves unreservedly. We can't underestimate the impact that family, culture, race, classism and all of these outer experiences have on the true acceptance of ourselves and by those around us, but it's the acceptance you feel on the inside that is going to lead you to the right path, whether you call yourself a lesbian or not. And first my lesbian label helped me to establish who I was in life, and to an extent it still does that. But ultimately who I am, how I treat people and what I do for my community is more important to me than any label I can give myself. I'm just chuffed that I get to be your lesbian big sister, queer or not.

Chapter 8

To Scissor or Not to Scissor?

et is what I thought the first time I touched someone else's vagina. I was taken aback, aghast, actually. I didn't know where to put my fingers, which angle I was supposed to be at, what bit was what, and my fingertips were slipping and sliding all over the place, like trying to catch an ice cube. The clitoris was evading my every move. It was, in my mind, the worst fumble of all time. It went absolutely nowhere and from that moment on, I was convinced I was terrible at sex. Being fifteen, I could have been a little kinder to myself, but from that moment on and for longer than I should have been, I was (I hate to admit it) a pillow princess. It wasn't for lack of wanting to reciprocate! But the trauma of my first vaginal experience had knocked my confidence so hard that I was too scared to jump back in the saddle for some time to come.

For my kudos, mainly, I'd like to state here that I'm not *actually* bad in bed. Ask around, people will tell you! But it took me a good couple of years, and a lot of sex, to realize

I wasn't totally useless in the bedroom, after all. Before you 'do it', sex is a scary thing, being intimate with someone is a scary thing and, first time or not, we all have moments of self-doubt. It's normal. And it's easier to feel like this because the sex education we receive growing up is solely for the premise of not falling pregnant, with absolutely no diversity in which genitals go where. More of this to come, but for now let's ease into things here. With the many gorgeous vaginas I've been lucky enough to experience, and all of the dalliances I've had, there are a few universal things that help to make intimate experiences incredible for both (or more) of you.

I'm going to refer to the vulva a lot during this chapter. Mainly because I have one myself, and those are the genitals that I've experienced mostly throughout my life as a lesbian woman. However, it's important to say that not all women have vulvas, and not all people who have vulvas are women. Please know that first, if you have, or are attracted to, any variation of the genetic anatomy that I'm referencing, all of what I'm talking about can be applied to you in some way. And second, your body deserves to be loved and touched and is a valid, sexy one.

Understanding how to pleasure your own body is the first step to knowing how to pleasure someone else's. Self-pleasure, thankfully, is becoming less and less stigmatized, but there is still a sense of taboo around the topic, especially for women. We know men touch themselves; hell, they can't leave themselves alone, but women? Touching themselves?! It's shocking! Well let me tell you now, it ain't. The majority of us are touching ourselves just as much as men are. It doesn't mean we're promiscuous, sluts or nymphomaniacs, it means we're human and self-pleasure is one of life's great joys, okay?

So what does masturbation look like first and foremost? Well it comes in so many different forms. It's not always sexy or even particularly sexual, which I know sounds bizarre, but there are a lot of different states of mind we can be in when we touch ourselves. Sometimes yes, we're feeling really turned on and just want to reach orgasm as quickly as possible. But it can also be comforting to masturbate; it can help induce sleep; it can be something that makes us feel safe and at home in ourselves; it relieves stress; the list goes on. Exploring masturbation is so useful for getting to know how you like to be touched, what sensations you enjoy and what gets you aroused. Being able to tap into your own sexual appetite is going to be so important when having sex with someone else, because if you don't know what you like, how the hell do you expect someone else to? So whatever you've been told, whatever internalized feelings of shame you have about masturbation, I'm giving you full, unadulterated permission to go forth and wank. Let it be your homework for this chapter if you like! It's a natural part of being a human, but if you're still feeling a bit naughty, do it for your health and well-being. The hormones produced during orgasm (oxytocin and nitric oxide) help to make you feel more energized, balance out your hormones and also help to maintain regular periods. #justsaying.

Speaking of which, let's talk about orgasms for a second, because whilst yes, it's wonderful to reach climax during sex or self-pleasure, it's not the be all and end all (pardon the pun). An orgasm is both a physical and psychological response. It's not just how the area is being aroused physically; a lot has to happen in the mind, and so being relaxed and comfortable is a huge part of being able to reach climax. Alongside that, not everyone *can* reach orgasm. Some people simply can't and there are so many different reasons that feed in to that. Those who are asexual, experience gender dysphoria, are on medication or have poor mental health might have a harder time reaching orgasm, so it's not a given for everybody. I think the best way to get there, if it *is* going to happen, is by letting an orgasm be a wonderful little bonus, a lottery win, if you will. The more we focus on the orgasm, the more we're likely to chase it away, and if you've experienced that before, you know exactly what I'm talking about. Take the pressure off and just let yourself be present in the pleasure. If it's gonna happen, it'll happen!

Now before we dive headfirst into the wonderful world of sex, we gotta make sure we're healthy and STI free. If you think women who have sex with women or people who have vulva on vulva sex are at a lower risk of catching a sexually transmitted infection, you're wrong. I don't want to scare you or take the fun out of sex, but like all things in life, there are things to consider when getting your thrills. Women can catch STIs such as herpes, genital warts and chlamydia when exchanging bodily fluids with another person, and any one-on-one contact such as oral sex or using the same hand when touching yourself and then your partner can put you at risk. In the heat of the moment, sex can go anywhere as long as it's consensual, so getting a sexual health check regularly is important. There are so many misconceptions when it comes to sexual health; for example, just because there's no penis involved doesn't mean there are no STIs going around. Also, HIV is actually more common in women than in men, which for so long has been stereotyped as a 'gay male disease'. So being on top of things, using condoms on sex toys, using dental dams when giving and receiving oral sex with new partners, and other safe practices, are so important to maintaining a happy and healthy sex life.

Meet Venus...

I'm Venus, my pronouns are she/her and I identify as pansexual.

Do you remember the *Kim Possible* Disney cartoon? I'd always be so excited to get home from school to watch TV because I loved watching her. The way her hair moved and her figure were so sexy to me, and I loved how it was animated. I soon noticed I had a strong attraction towards girls and couldn't wait to get home and watch more female-focused shows like *That's So Raven* or *Lizzie McGuire*. While I was growing up, my mum played ice hockey, where ninety per cent of the team was lesbian. So I consistently watched women kiss each other, hold hands and develop beautiful, healthy relationships in front of me. So to me, that was so normal and desirable; however, being gay wasn't something I felt I could ever express.

I was always intrigued by girls, and I've always been fascinated by the female form. So I was inquisitive growing up, and it wasn't until I met my best friend in school, who was also gay, that I started to open up about my feelings and fantasies. However, I was still very confused about labels until I was twenty-eight. I didn't feel connected to the word bisexual, so for many years, I felt pretty confused about my identity and how to fit into the queer space. Then, with social media, I began meeting more people within that community, and someone mentioned pansexual. So I went away and looked into it and thought, 'Wow, that is who I am.' It is all about connection, and I'm big on energy. It's about feeling something regardless of how you identify. And to me, that was the pinnacle moment in knowing how I identify.

I didn't start experimenting with the opposite sex until my thirties, and for many years I thought to myself, 'How can I give myself a label if I haven't explored it or done it?' But just because you haven't done something doesn't mean you can't put yourself in that category. So you're no less valid. Looking back, I am glad I took my time and didn't rush into exploring anything out of fear of not living up to expectations or labels.

When it comes to sex, being sure of what you like is always a work in progress and forever evolving, but knowing what you want and also having the courage to go for it is all part of the fun. Just make sure it's on your terms and consensual. There's real power in being comfortable in yourself, and communicating what you want is the most important thing. However, you also have to listen. You must be a good listener because it's a two-way street, right? Many people struggle with the fear of somebody saying, 'No, I'm not comfortable with that.' Please don't take offence to it, and don't be afraid to say it back. There are always ways to compromise, especially when it comes to sex!

A noncompromise, however, should always be your sexual health. This should always be a priority if you are sexually active. Unfortunately, there is a common misconception that if you're a vulva owner only sleeping with other vulva owners, you don't need to look out for STIs. However, women who have sex with other women can pass on or get STIs. So test regularly, and don't be afraid to ask for your partner's latest results or if they are even testing. Always safety first, and peace of mind goes a long way.

The biggest thing that's helped me on my queer journey so far has been surrounding myself with people in the community and learning from them. Pushing myself outside of the box and not worrying about what everyone else thinks. I wish I had done that so much sooner. I am also a big fan of therapy, and I have spent a lot of time figuring out who I am as an individual and finding my voice. It has benefited me in more ways than one and supported me on this journey of self-discovery.

Venus Libido

Now that we're masturbating freely, let's get into the juiciness of involving other naked bodies, shall we? You might have come across the terms top, bottom or switch, which, I won't lie, I think we stole from the gays. They're phrases that determine whether you predominantly give (a top), receive (a bottom) or do a bit of both (a switch). Being a top doesn't mean that you exclusively give, and likewise for a bottom with receiving, but the terms help to establish what we're into, sexually. Take them, much like we do all other labels, with a pinch of salt, as they're not set in stone and can change depending on mood, time of the month, the partner you're with and so on. But generally two tops together might find themselves in a bit of a power struggle in the bedroom, and two bottoms might never even get out of their clothes, and so generally, knowing your own and somebody else's preference helps you to decide whether you might be compatible in the bedroom. I definitely classed myself as a 'bottom' when I first came out and needed to be handheld into the world of vulva-on-vulva sex. Whereas, nowadays, I sit firmly in the 'switch' category.

For a long time, I thought my lesbian gene was broken because (and I've never talked about this before) I didn't like going down on someone. I didn't enjoy giving oral sex. It kind of freaked me out, tbh! It's someone's vulva...in my mouth! It actually made me question my entire lesbian identity because I thought, 'I should definitely like doing this if I'm gay, right?' It took me a while to realize that I did, actually, enjoy giving oral sex, but only if I was really into the person. It's such an intimate thing to do and I realized that one of my boundaries is that unless we're in 'the feels', I'm not doing it. All of us have different boundaries around different types of sex and that's the exciting thing about it. It can be so varied and explorative and it's a wonderful feeling being in control of your pleasure.

Of course now I know that even if I never gave head in my life, that doesn't make me any less of a lesbian; being gay isn't about what you're doing with your mouth, after all. There are different types of sex, different types of connections and just because you enjoy something with one person doesn't mean that you will want to do that with everyone you're intimate with. Sex is very personal; it's different from partner to partner and is about what you're comfortable exploring and enjoying with another person. Although I really enjoy casual sex, it taught me that there are stark differences between the type of sex I have when there are feelings involved and when I'm there simply for the thrill of the moment. By my mid-twenties, I'd gained more sexual confidence and had really settled into who I was, and so my sexual preferences began to change and evolve, too. Once I stopped worrying about what I was doing and what the other person thought,

I could think about what I wanted and enjoyed doing to someone else.

I told you that I grew up a people pleaser, and that behaviour transferred into my romantic relationships, too. It wasn't until I started shedding that persona and looked deeply at who I was that I began to feel more able to explore different types of sex. Putting myself first rather than simply pleasing the other person. To really 'get' sex, you also have to shed the idea of what you think sex is. For a lot of us, the first experience we have of it is seeing it through porn, which, first and foremost, is designed for a male audience. That means that what we see is a total performance: women throwing themselves about making over-the-top noises and practically orgasming after one quick flick of the clitoris. So seeing porn as our first point of reference for what sex should look like is really confusing and takes some time to unlearn. That said, porn itself isn't the problem. It's very natural to want to watch people having sex and there are some amazing female-owned production companies that are making porn accessible for women and queer people. Just make sure that if you do want to enjoy porn, go forth and do so but please pay for it; sex workers have bills to pay, too.

The sex education I *wish* I'd had growing up would have taught me that whilst yes, sex between a man and a woman can lead to babies, it's also meant to be fun! It's one of life's greatest pleasures, and as long as it's safe and consensual it is something for everyone to enjoy if they want to. For it to be a quality sexual experience it has to include things like communication, relaxation, trust, eye contact and really tuning into the other person or people. Sadly, my sex ed teacher just taught us how to whack a condom on a banana and so

I've devised my own small syllabus of what leads to great sex between anyone you choose to 'do it' with:

- Communicate beforehand – We don't have to be mute about sex. We can, and you absolutely should, talk about what you like, where your boundaries are and what really gets you off. Sex is a vulnerable thing, so learning to be open is going to be key in having the very best experience. This counts for *during* sex, too. I'd rather you tell me exactly where you want to be touched rather have me than guess and not be hitting 'the spot'; that doesn't help either of us. You might feel like you can't direct someone because you don't want to hurt their feelings or make them feel like they're 'not doing it right'. You might feel embarrassed to say what you want and, honestly, we all are at first. But I'm telling you now, after having had a lot of sex over the years, a little bit of guidance always goes down well. It only helps to improve the sexual experience and deepens the connection between you.

- Take it slow – I know 'the horn' can sometimes take over and make you feel like you simply *must* have sex right this second or you'll combust, but starting off slowly is never a bad idea. Taking your time to make that sexual connection with someone is going to go a lot smoother than if you're going at it a hundred miles per hour. The misconception is to rush in, like a bull in a china shop, and head straight for the genitals. But taking your time to explore your partner's entire body is a really connecting thing and targets the 'pleasure nerves'. Think Monica from *Friends*, explaining the seven erogenous zones to Chandler: no one wants it straight in the seven! Slow and gentle touch encourages and enhances sexual hormones and helps to build up the sexual energy between you, so take. Your. Time.

- Listen to the other person – We've talked about communication and whilst yes, talking about what you want is going to lead to a better time in bed, are you actually *listening* to what the other person wants, too? Listening with your ears and also with your eyes, looking at and understanding body language, taking cues from your partner by listening to their breath, the noises that they're making and so on. Listening really means immersing yourself in the experience entirely, going where your partner goes and recognizing where to explore, when to stop and where to switch it up.

- Don't take it so seriously – Sex is meant to be fun! The majority of what we see of sex in the media and through porn is that it's either sexy and mysterious or wildly passionate and raunchy. Of course sex *can* be those things, but much like Instagram vs reality, sex irl should most importantly be fun. Self-conscious or performative sex is the worst, so let go and play around, don't be afraid to laugh, stop worrying about whether your boobs look good from this angle or whether you've shaved or not. Trust me, everyone's just happy to be there! Sex is the best when we let our inner imagination run free and get out of our heads, so throw out the rule book and lose your inhibitions. I promise you, it's worth it.

- Patience – Much like figuring out your personal style, finding the perfect moisturizer for your skin type or the best Chinese takeout in your area, finding the right sexual partner for you could take some time! Not every sexual encounter you have is going to be the best sex you've ever had, and that's okay. Sometimes you can have incredible chemistry with someone on a date only to find that in the bedroom, it's awkward as hell. You might even find you have the best sex with someone you don't actually like! Sexual chemistry is a prankster like that sometimes. You win some, you lose some, but honestly you can always have a fun and connective experience if you take into consideration all of the above.

Bonus tip: If you've had a drink or two, firstly let's be aware of what consensual sex is and the potential impact having drunk sex can have. And secondly, under the influence, your orgasm is very unlikely gonna happen! Don't chafe yourself in pursuit of it. Get some sleep and try again in the morning, when you're sober.

Meet Skylar...

I'm Skylar, my pronous are she/they and I use the following labels: queer, bisexual, demisexual, asexual, grey asexual and aegosexual.

I grew up attending a Scientology private school in a small town in Oregon, USA. I knew I was queer from the age of six, but I saw how people who were read as queer were bullied and knew very early on that in order to survive in my environment I needed to work as hard as I could to fit in. I internalized an immense amount of the homophobia and misogyny that I was surrounded by and truly began to hate myself. It was extremely difficult for me to form friendships with girls. I didn't understand how to interact with them and I was terrified to talk to the ones I had crushes on, and so I formed friendships with boys and became an 'I'm not like other girls' girl. It was a very sad time.

I first discovered the label 'asexual' on Tumblr in my twenties and after reading the description, I immediately started crying. Not only had my feelings and experiences been described in detail, but I realized that other people felt this way, too. It was like discovering myself and finding a community all at once. It was really beautiful.

Labels were extremely important to me when I first came out, but now, not so much. I know myself so much better and feel secure in my queerness and my existence as a whole, and I've formed such a beautiful community around me and see how varied and beautiful the spectrum of queerness is. The important thing to remember about labels is that they're descriptive, not prescriptive. They're not rigid guidelines to follow; they're tools we use to describe our lived experience and to find other people who share those experiences.

As a bisexual femme, my identity is constantly being erased, misunderstood or fetishized. If I date someone who reads as a woman, I'm a lesbian, and if I date someone who reads as a man, then I'm straight. If I date multiple genders at once, I'm a greedy, slutty, bisexual trope. I learned very quickly that there was no winning, but I don't live my life for other people. My queerness is complicated and ever-changing, but it is mine and the only person who needs to understand it is me.

Living outside of a big city, my dating pool is extremely small. It's incredibly isolating attempting to date or even to just exist in a world where the vast majority of people around you do not share the same philosophies on sex, love, romance, family, etc. Dating as a solo polyamorous person adds another level of complexity, and even some polyamorous people misunderstand what solo polyamory is. To monogamous people, I'm seen as a commitment-phobe, or promiscuous, so I feel like I'm constantly having to explain and defend my philosophies on relationships to people, when I owe that to no one.

I still have to remind myself that there is nothing 'wrong' with me as far as my asexuality goes. It's often compared to celibacy, which is a conscious choice made by people who still experience sexual attraction, but I'm not choosing to be asexual. This is who I am. I'm a proud slut who dresses provocatively, which leads people to ask why would I dress that way if I don't want to have sex. My answer is that I dress the way that I do because it makes me feel good and I'm hot; there's no other reason.

I'm extremely proud to be as visibly and vocally queer as I am. I'm living a life teenage me could have never envisioned for herself. I am the person now that I desperately needed in my life when I was growing up.

Skylar Mundy

Then, babe, once you've got the basics nailed, it's time to go from beginner lesbian to intermediate lesbian.

The first sex toy I bought was from Ann Summers, the only sexually focused shop that's 'acceptable' to enter on a British high street without getting the side eye from seventy-year-old Brenda. Lingerie is placed at the front of the store and at the back, it's a party! After building up the courage to go in for my first purchase, I walked out of there, proud as punch, with the three-inch gold-coated bullet vibrator. That is, until I got home and basically burnt my clitoris off. Jeez, that was a lesson learned. I lost all sensation in my nether regions and felt like I had a teeny, tiny razor burn on the hood of my clitoris for about three days. Ouch! Suffice to say, I haven't used one since, but it didn't destroy my sex toy curiosity altogether.

Once the disappointment of the bullet wore off, I opted for a rabbit. This is a toy that blew up in the mid 2000s because it was featured in *Sex and the City*, and so I thought that was an appropriate next step for me. The rabbit had a dildo – a penis portion – which you penetrate yourself with, and then a rabbit-ears-shaped vibrating portion, which stimulates your clitoris at the same time. I did get a bit more use out of that one, but self-penetration, I learned, just doesn't really do it for me when I'm masturbating. A lot of people with vulvas don't enjoy penetrative sex altogether, which is why it's important to communicate as much as possible and never assume what people are into. These days I'm all about the air pulse stimulation vibrators, the ones that feel like genuine head. And because it's been my main side boo for the last five years, I have to give a shout out to the Satisfyer Curvy 1+, which blows my mind, every, single, time. The only problem I have with it is that I think I might be addicted... No, really, please remember that toys should be adding and enhancing to your pleasure and not replacing genuine connection, okay?

It can be overwhelming when you start to look for toys because there are so many out there, and so I'd definitely suggest making the whole process a fun experience by looking with your partner, date or pals. Venus, who you heard from earlier, is a true sex toy connoisseur so she's worth a follow to find out about the very best products on the market. Just remember to take the pressure off and what's most important is that, and say it with me, 'Sex is fun!' You know what else is fun? Strap-ons. Advanced-level lesbian sex, activated.

The most notorious sex toy in the lesbian world is the strap-on. It is a harness that's worn around the waist and thighs and holds a dildo/penetrative sex toy. The stereotype is that the masc wears the strap and the femme receives, but trust me, masc-presenting lesbians can often be far more 'bottom' than you'd think. Never assume someone's role with the strap-on and use your newly improved powers of communication to get clear about how everyone feels. It can be nerve-wracking wearing one and can feel awkward not being able to feel exactly where the dildo is going. It takes a bit of getting used to for sure, not to mention you'll need your strength and stamina if you're on top! If you're receiving, it can sometimes stir up an emotional response – it's a powerful sexual act after all – so make sure you have time for some self-care afterwards. Size, colour and the harness material are all things to take into consideration, and again, choosing your strap-on should be a fun experience! So shop around and take your time to find the right one for you. Indulge your inner Goldilocks, if you will.

Practically, I'd suggest opting for an easy to clean material for your harness and a nonporous dildo to be as on top of your sexual health as possible. It's worth investing in a good quality one so that you don't have to spend unnecessarily. I remember wearing a strap-on for the first time and feeling totally embarrassed thinking that I looked stupid and had no idea what I was doing. But trust me, if men can do it, so can you, babe. The only thing I *can't* tell you, and I don't think any lesbian can, is how to step in and out of a strap-on harness with grace and dignity. The answer to that evades me to this day.

I feel like by now, you get my drift about taking it slow and being communicative when it comes to sex, but as someone who is no stranger to a one-night stand, I have to advocate for my sexually adventurous queers, too. Of course we're bearing all of the above in mind, but losing your inhibitions, being playful with our sexual encounters and being liberated queers is also really fun, too. I have always loved connecting with people in a sexual way; I don't need to know someone's middle name to want to go to bed with them. And whilst in my early twenties my love for bed-hopping got me into a few sticky situations that I could have avoided, for the most part I'm glad to have had fun with my sex life. I remember going to my first all-female sex party, full of nerves, and braving it alone. I soon found myself laid on a bed with six other women having the time of our lives, albeit a little cramped. It's liberating to be free with your sexuality, but ultimately it's about personal choice and what you feel comfortable with.

From sex parties to sex-less, it wouldn't be right to end this chapter without talking about one of the biggest killers of lesbian relationships globally, and that's lesbian bed death. LBD is when the sex dies out, leading to a sexless relationship and frequently, a break up. Women aren't fuelled with testosterone like men are, which means sex can so easily fall by the wayside in lesbian relationships. Combine that with two menstrual cycles and fluctuating hormones and there's a lot to contend with. Of course some long-term couples have little or no sex and are perfectly happy with that, not forgetting our asexual peers, too. But if this happens unwillingly, you gotta just bite the bullet and talk about it. The sooner the better. Talk about things with no pressure, judgement or accusations and with the idea of coming to a shared solution. We're told that regular sex is 'normal' and 'natural' and therefore not having *any* makes us feel like there's something wrong. But there is no 'normal' amount. It's really about what works for you, so be kind to one another, and chat it out before it's too late.

In the next chapter we're going to be talking more about the power of communication to improve our interpersonal relationships, but taking it to the office. Although actually, I might just be giving you some role play ideas there. But lastly, on the topic of sex, it really is and can be so great. It's a vast world to explore and with so many possibilities, fantasies, partners and experiences to be had. I encourage you to go for it, with care and well-being at the centre, but with a sense of fun and exploration too because you deserve to be sexually fulfilled. Remember to respect each encounter that you have and don't be afraid to open up with those around you. Talk about, laugh about and celebrate your sexual experiences with your peers, because we're in a time when we're more able to do so than ever. Women have been taught for centuries that sex is for men, that it's a service, that we should be 'good at it' but we shouldn't enjoy it too much. That we should be slutty virgins, frigid hoes and all manner of contradictory things. But sexual shame is cancelled; it's fast becoming a thing of the past and rightfully so, because all of us deserve sexual autonomy.

And finally, to answer the chapter's question. Yes, lesbians do, in fact, scissor. And I highly recommend giving it a go!

Chapter 9

Lez Get to Work!

Back in 2014, here in the UK, it was decided that same-sex couples *do* deserve the same rights as straight people after all, and that we could marry one another, officially. Woohoo! And so lots of queer people who had undergone a civil partnership then made arrangements to say 'I do' once more, and hung their marriage licences on the mantelpiece. It's a victory hard won and a fantastic step forward in the fight for equality, and a little later in this chapter, we're going to hear from the two incredible women who began the movement to pass that bill. But whilst not all of us want to get married (each to their own), all of us do in fact need to hold down a job. Gay or not, we all need to earn a living and so, actually, for a large portion of the queer community, it's our workplace rights that are more important to us than whether or not we can walk down the aisle. And since straight people still argue against our continued fight for equality with 'You're allowed to get married, what more do you want?', well, Karen, let me tell you.

A fraction of our workplace rights is protected in some parts of the world, yet there is persistent discrimination against the LGBTQ+ community from so many different angles, and so the office can be one of the most high-stakes spaces for us to navigate. Take the US, for example: there are no federal laws to protect employees from discrimination surrounding sexuality and gender, and whilst laws vary from state to state, it makes being out at work in the US a very vulnerable and risky decision. In fact, a Human Rights Campaign report states that in the US, 46 per cent of LGBTQ+ workers say that they're not out at work even though it's proven that when workers can show up as their authentic selves, they're more productive (duh!).[3] The same report also found that the main reason people don't report negative comments that they hear about LGBTQ+ people to senior management is because A) they don't think anything will be done about it, and B) they don't want to cause friction with their work colleagues. Ugh, I hate that so many of us are being backed into this corner.

Similarly, here in the UK, Stonewall (an LGBTQ+ human rights charity) discovered back in 2018, one third of LGBTQ+ staff have hidden their identity at work, and that one in ten Black, Asian and minority ethnic LGBTQ+ employees have been physically attacked by customers or colleagues.[4] Those figures are staggering, and it's heartbreaking to think that so many of us are going about our lives inauthentically, in fear and at the risk of both verbal and physical assault. Particularly when we're just out here trying to do our jobs and to earn a living. However, there are some countries around the world that are much farther forward in their acceptance of our community. In Madrid in Spain, for example, discrimination laws protecting LGB people have been in place since 1995, and legislation supporting transgender rights (particularly around the right to self-identify) are some of the most progressive in the world. It's not all bad news, you see. See you in Madrid?

The start of this chapter sounds a bit bloody depressing to be honest, even to a silver lining kinda gal like myself. The facts and figures don't exactly spark hope for a happy and fulfilled work life, but it's important to know where things stand so that we know where we *don't* want to be. I promise that by the time you move on to Chapter 10, you'll be left with a sense of boundless opportunity, knowing that this is just the start of history in the making. I want you to look at those figures above and let them spur you into action, the action of feeling like you're a part of something bigger than yourself. Know that there are queer people globally who face the same issue of workplace worry. But that just like in every other part of your life, your queerness doesn't have to hold you back. And in fact, say it with me, 'It won't.'

I was twenty-two when I ran away to North Devon, to the British seaside, away from my marriage and my fear of not knowing what I wanted to do with my life. I took a job as a singer at a holiday resort there and whilst it sounds glamorous, the truth is you had to live on site for the job, and so when I arrived I was escorted to a caravan (a trailer) that was clearly over one hundred years old. The furniture was dusty and stained, it had gaps around the window frames, so a constant draft ran through it, and you literally had to shower over the toilet. It was a femme gal's nightmare! But I put on my big girl pants and started to clean up the hovel that I now called home, ripping out some of the ugly interior, banging a few nails in here and there, and I won't lie, I was really getting my teeth into DIY lesbian life. Now you might be thinking, 'Helen, what the hell has this got to do with being out at work?', and to that I say, stay with me...

I headed off to rehearsals that afternoon and immediately was summoned to the general manager's office. News of my

DIY activities had spread and had not been met with much kindness. Now, I'd heard about the GM but was yet to meet her, and apparently she was a nightmare boss: strict, hard to please and never smiled at anyone. But what I'd also heard about her was that she was very, very gay. So I felt both intrigued and nervous, as I pushed my boobs up in my bra, whacked on some fresh lip gloss and marched into her office ready for a showdown.

She was so fit I could barely look at her. Tall and masc with dark hair and an air of authority that was both terrifying and utterly sexy, she was right up my alley, gang. As I predicted, she was none too impressed about my redesign of the caravan, but I stood my ground (even though you could have mopped me off of the floor at this point) and I told her to come and take a look for herself. I said that if she would live in it, in its dirty, mucky, uninhabitable state, that I'd put it all back the way that I found it and she'd hear no more from me. So she walked down to the caravan with me there and then, and after a quick inspection she sent round not one but an entire team of maintenance men to fix it up for me! I was victorious! The funny thing is that I only ended up living in that caravan for about two weeks because, of course, from that moment on we were smitten, began dating immediately and U-Hauled in a matter of days. My work–life balance couldn't have been better. In this instance, being 'out at work' proved to be very much in my favour.

My industry is one of the more inclusive ones in terms of sexuality. After all, the world of entertainment is largely a diverse one, where gay men rule and the straight community lap it up eagerly (I'm still waiting for more lesbian representation, of course, but I'm working on remedying that every day). Whilst that makes it easier to be myself, as a freelancer

I work with so many different people, brands and teams that I find myself having to come out a lot! We talked about this in Chapter 2, about how coming out isn't this one glorious moment of stepping out of a dingy, cobweb-filled closet and into a shining rainbow of light and acceptance (sadly, 'cause that sounds fun!). It's the small things like correcting people when they refer to your partner as 'he', referring to LGBTQ+ media that you consume in conversation or clearing your throat when you hear a homophobic comment being thrown around, unintentionally or not. It can be draining to constantly be reminded of your other-ness, and to have to speak about your sexuality time and time again.

What *is* exciting is that more and more businesses, particularly those of a larger scale, are implementing workplace protections for the community. As we move further and further into the digital age, whether by choice or not, companies simply *must* diversify and implement inclusion or face the wrath of the internet. The wrath of the queers isn't one to be sneered at, as no one stands up for one another more than the queers do, honey. Now of course, we'd like it to be a conscious choice, a decision of care to put those safeguarding measures in place, but as we know from our ancestors before us, every step forward is a win in the fight for total equality and acceptance, and the more this is implemented on a global scale and normalized as part of corporate culture, the quicker we can get on and do our damn jobs without fear or persecution. Can I get an amen?

I interviewed for a presenting role in the tech space some years ago, which had started out brilliantly, and I could feel that the guy sitting opposite me was impressed. We rounded things up by hashing it out about hours, salary and when I could start. Then all of a sudden he whipped the rug from under my feet, so nonchalantly that I felt like I'd been back-handed, and said, 'Oh and by the way, you'll need to tone down the gay.' Yes. This straight, white (and frankly ugly) balding man told me that to get the role I'd need to be less 'openly gay', as a lot of his clients are men, and they wouldn't like it. Now, I don't consider myself to be a violent person, Famalam, but in my mind I left that guy with a nosebleed and a particularly sore pair of testicles. But ultimately, Dave (let's call him Dave), a near fifty-year-old dude residing in the tech space, was simply saying what a large proportion of businessmen think, infuriatingly so. His intention when saying that wasn't to offend me – he was far too ignorant to know that it was offensive – he was truly just being hon-est. Sadly, the world being led by straight, white, old men doesn't always make our lives easy, so what are our options? You could either start your own business and pave a rain-bow-coloured way in whichever field you so choose, or you can work in these companies and make them see and hear you for being the incredibly hard-working and, frankly, ir-replaceable member of the workforce that you are. Sounds oversimplified, I know, but there are more actionable steps to come, I promise. But my point is that, either way, there is opportunity for both the community and you to win.

Making the decision to be out at work depends on lots of different factors like how safe you feel, how important it is to you, your mental well-being and so on. It can also be a hard decision to make if you don't have any queer colleagues (that you know of) to speak to or feel connected with. For some of those who are gender nonconforming or diverse, being closeted at work is the only option and can have significant detrimental effects. What I do know is that when you hide something about yourself, it doesn't usually bode well for reaching your potential. I mean, who isn't going to be able to better focus on the job at hand when they're not hiding who they are, even more so for the trans community when the gender affirmation they receive from those around them can be, quite literally, lifesaving? Research has found that leading a double life – being out in your private life but not at work – increases social stress and depression.[5] Studies have also shown that people who are out at work are happier with their careers and view both their companies and colleagues more favourably compared to their closeted peers. When we can be, the psychological value of being out is so incredibly positive and impactful in us being able to live that fulfilled life we're after. However, saying that, it's a two-way street, right? The more welcoming and positive workplaces are, the easier it's going to be for us to be ourselves.

You can tell a lot about a company's values, its level of inclusivity and the internal mindset from the outset by their application system. If they don't offer gender-inclusive options when filling out an application for the job, then the chances are it's not going to get much better than that when you're actually *working* there. Research suggests that, in the past, employers have been more likely to view applications from the LGBTQ+ community unfavourably, and in a way, I think it's actually done us a favour.[6] Of course we should be allowed fair game at any job that takes our fancy, but the more we take control of where we commit our skills and talent, the bigger an impact their lack of diversity and inclusivity will have. The STEM (science, technology, engineering and mathematics) industries, for example, are said to have lost 120,000 LGBTQ+-identifying employees over the last year for their lack of inclusivity. On the other hand, the number of startups and LGBTQ+-specific businesses in that space has grown.[7] Ultimately, what we can say to employers these days is, if you aren't doing your bit to include and protect us, we're not wasting our time and talents on you any longer. The future is queer inclusive, and businesses, I believe, are beginning to understand the power of allyship.

I'm pretty sure I got my radio show on the BBC, in part, because I'm a lesbian. I mean obviously, I'm phenomenal at my job (if you don't know, you should get to know!), but at the time the pressure was on for them not to hire another straight, white man. Did I feel tokenized? I guess I did, to an extent. But did it allow me to represent my community in a fantastic way to 200,000 listeners a night? Yes. I was only doing what straight, white men have done for centuries and made the system work for me. To be honest, it felt like my turn! Frankly, I'll take the inclusion any day of the week, even if it was partly performative, because all businesses have to start somewhere and the impact it has on diversity and inclusion is phenomenal. I believe that by me doing that show, it did more for the LGBTQ+ community than had I turned it down for feeling like I'd been hired on bias. If businesses are hiring based on diversity, I'm ready to cash in!

Meet Lucy and Stella...

I'm Lucy, my pronouns are she/her, and I identify as a gay woman, a lesbian. My wife Stella, Stell for short, doesn't do labels but her pronouns are she/her.

L: We should never have met! It was a unique meeting, a unique feeling and we have a unique love. As soon as we met, I knew there was something very different about how we both felt; we were instantly drawn to each other. Living so far away from each other, it wasn't easy and it wasn't convenient. But we had an uncontrollable want to be near each other and so I drove the one hundred miles to meet Stell in her hometown and the rest is history.

S: At the time it wasn't legal for same-sex couples to marry here in the UK and we battled as a couple with friends and family to be accepted. We wanted to make sure 'family' would never keep us apart legally and wanted protection for each other if we got sick, security for the dreams we'd built together and so on. Did we wish to get married because we were in love? Of course! But there was the fundamental injustice that we didn't have the same rights as our peers. And so, we set to work. We created a media campaign, the MRS&MRS campaign first, and the MR&MR campaign shortly followed. Initially it was all about drumming up awareness of the marriage equality bill and making sure our community and everyone knew what Parliament was proposing, enabling the same rights to same-sex and heterosexual couples.

With both of us at the time in the fashion editorial arena, we reached multiple audiences sharing our truth, and before we knew it, the following grew, and it grew quickly. We marched, petitioned and rallied to make it known that we wouldn't give up until we could legally marry one another, and finally knew that we'd caused an effect when the Home Office called, summoning us the following day.

L: It was one of the best yet scariest moments of our lives together. We were questioned on our intentions, on why we had started the campaign and how we had got so much traction so quickly. We told them our story, sharing our fight to simply be who we are and to be together. Incredibly we were asked to work with the Home Office on the marriage equality bill which passed in 2013. We were some of the first to know the outcome and did days of protesting outside the Houses of Parliament. We were married as soon as the bill was passed and we could legally book it.

S: It was a privilege to be recognized and to play a pivotal part in this huge moment in history. To be handed the new legislation documents to look over was a surreal moment. It felt like all of our Christmases and birthdays had come at once. It was always bigger than 'us'; it was for everyone who loved someone of the same sex and a message to every person growing up that marriage could be for you. That you could dream about marriage just like your peers or siblings do. That you can have the same rights, start a family and be in a legal partnership, if you wish. It was all about enabling the freedom of choice. It was an honour to work on it and ultimately, it changed our lives as it did for others.

Lucy London and Stella

Let's get to the actionables, shall we? The first thing to do if you're considering coming out at work, or when taking a new job, is to learn about the company's policies and stance towards LGBTQ+ rights. What framework do they have in place to protect you, to help you feel a sense of community, and what measures are in place to protect you if those boundaries are crossed? This is something that can be raised at the interview stage if you feel comfortable to do so, or it can be researched online beforehand, even by reaching out to current/past employees and seeking their experiences via platforms like LinkedIn. This isn't always the easiest way to go about understanding a workplace's culture, but it's often the truest representation that you'll find, and so it's well worth doing some detective work. Using social media and an old-fashioned Google search might just save you walking into a job that could leave you traumatized.

You may have faced, or are even currently facing, discriminatory behaviour in the workplace because of your sexuality. Big or small, these things can be emotionally draining and scary to navigate. Microaggressions are usually the most common thing you'll face: everyday slights, put-downs or insults from others who are, often, unaware that they've said or done something offensive. They can be verbal, nonverbal, intentional or unintentional but because as a community we're more attuned to discrimination in general, we're much more likely to pick up on them and to report unjust behaviour. It's brave to speak out against injustice of any kind, particularly as women or gender-diverse humans; there's a lot to contend with. Opposing the pressure to play along, not to submit to male-validating culture and to report sexual misconduct of any kind is something women have been battling with for years. Sadly, LGBTQ+ women, especially those who identify as bisexual or nonmonogamous, experience more microaggressions than most and are most likely to hear sexist comments about their gender and have sexually explicit comments directed at them. Most of us can't afford to lose our jobs fighting for equality but with regards to all of the above, this is where knowing your rights and implementing safeguarding measures comes into play.

Whilst it's not your responsibility to teach or educate others, the workplace is somewhere where opinions, thoughts, personalities and identities collide, and so doing your best to be great communicators and advocates for the community is going to serve you well. Purposefully discriminatory behaviour should always be escalated without question, but microaggressions can sometimes be resolved with the person at hand if you have the emotional capacity to do so. Whether it's simply letting someone know they've upset or offended you, or helping them to correct their behaviour moving forwards, it's not always easy to fight the good fight day in, day out, but it's possible.

Alternatively, your HR department is there for a reason, they're there to support and protect you, so don't be afraid to use them. Reporting incidents should not only positively impact your own working life but will no doubt have a ripple effect for those around you or who come after you. I appreciate that it's not your job to be an activist in your workspace, but hopefully it's something that you feel proud to do regardless. However, I draw the line when it comes to Pride month. The month of June is sacred for the LGBTQ+ community, a thirty-day celebration of who we are and a chance for the spotlight to be shone on issues that we still face today. Going to HR about microaggressions I support, but being the token LGBTQ+ employee for the month of June absolutely not, unless you're being highly compensated to do so.

There's been a rise in businesses stepping up and showing support during Pride month over the last five years or so and, undisputedly, this has a positive impact on the lives of our community. When big brands stand with us, it acts as a loudspeaker to the world that LGBTQ+ people are worthy and loved and important. However, if it's only to be able to say, 'we're LGBTQ+ friendly' without doing anything more than performative rainbow washing, that's a real problem and we're not settling for it any longer. If you're inclusive, you're doing the work of making change and room for diverse people from the ground up, and we want to see it. A lot of businesses are scared to get things wrong and so use LGBTQ+ employees to showcase their inclusivity without having year-round processes or action plans in place. The labour of creating a more LGBTQ+-inclusive workplace shouldn't fall on you. However, if you want to be involved, aiding in creating diversity and inclusion practices can certainly bring about good, so long as it's not at the expense of your own time or emotions.

There are two things that you could champion in the workplace, from everyday impactful changes like diversifying bathroom facilities to included all gender options and ensuring systems are inclusive of all employees' potential genders to longer-term inclusivity action plans like supporting leave for transitioning colleagues, conscious inclusion training and creating safe reporting channels. These things can have a huge impact on a company's future success, after all, and making it psychologically safe for LGBTQ+ people and any member of a minority group, for that matter, to be out of the closet at work should be a priority for companies striving to retain their employees. This also extends to including queer employees in benefits like parental leave and inclusive pay packages, something to consider when reading the next chapter all about LGBTQ+ family life.

Whilst there is a correlation between being out and productivity in your work life, ultimately it's your decision. Ask yourself what living authentically looks like to you, and what the consequences of not getting to live that authentic life would be. Then it's up to you whether the consequences outweigh the importance of authenticity. There's no right or wrong, like with most things we do with regards to our sexuality, but if you are out in the workplace, there may well be highs and lows, there may well be some questionable conversations over the coffee machine with Gary from finance, but there will always be community. Community who love and understand you, the experiences you're having, and who are celebrating your bravery by putting yourself out there. Now, in the words of the great RuPaul, 'You betta WERK!'

Chapter 10

Queer Families & Their Intricacies

I don't want to be a parent. I thought I did when I was younger, and I always said that I felt in my gut that if I ended up having kids, I'd have twins. I still believe to this day that if I *were* to give birth, two little babies would come flying out of me. I can't have been born with this hip width for any other reason! But what I look back and realize is that I didn't know any different then; I thought that everyone had kids because that's the narrative I grew up with and that's just what everyone did. Now? I know that it's my choice to abstain and instead be everyone's favourite gay aunt who spoils them at Christmas.

From the time we're born, unintentionally and ignorantly, we're sexualized. You've heard people say things like, 'She'll be fighting off all the boys' (ew), or you'll have seen videos of macho dads telling their little girls that they're not allowed a boyfriend until they're thirty. Again, ew! And don't even get me started on gender reveal parties. Blue is for boys and pink is for girls. With everything we know about gender fluidity, in the twenty-first century, has everyone lost their damn minds? And I ask myself when the homophobes get on their high horse about queer people having children, what makes them think *straight* people are so qualified in the first place?

Being a great parent isn't about gender, it's about doing your best to raise a human who has the life skills to see themselves into adulthood and beyond. Like, it's hard! The hardest thing in the world probably. And people just walk around thinking it's the inevitable next step, it's the final thing to be ticked off of their life list. No one walks around thinking, 'I'll give brain surgery a go today and see if it works out,' and parenting is literally 10,000 times harder than brain surgery. So why don't people take having kids as seriously? I'm exaggerating, obviously, and tangenting hard, I know. Ranting even? But this part of being queer, this particular prejudice that we face about having and raising children of our own, really pisses me off. And as a lesbian who doesn't even want kids, that's really saying something.

The argument that homophobes try to use is how important it is to be raised by two parents of the opposite gender. That children need both a man and a woman to raise them in order to grow into healthy, happy adults. Some (straight) people would rather see children in social care for their entire formative years than have same-sex couples be able to adopt, to give those children stability, safety and boundless love. They believe that children are at a disadvantage being raised by two women, and that men provide a different, indispensable set of parenting skills than women do. It's delusional homophobia to the point of utter ignorance, and what evidence do I have to suggest that they're wrong? Well, research literally proves that it's utter BS, for a start. Researchers have found no evidence of gender-based parenting abilities, with the partial exception of lactation, noting that very little about the gender of a parent has significance for children's psychological adjustment and social success. In fact, on average, two mothers tended to play with their children *more*, were less likely to use physical discipline and were less likely to raise children with chauvinistic attitudes.[8] So bite me, Karen.

My parents split up when I was seven, and whilst I was lucky to have both parents remain present in my life when they separated, the trauma I was left with from their broken relationship has had a huge impact on the person I've grown up to be. Thankfully I've had the capacity to learn and evolve into someone I'm proud of, and look, it wasn't their *fault*, they didn't purposefully traumatize me, but of course unhappy parents are going to have an impact on their children, and I'm not saying that two women wouldn't produce the same result. But just because you have a man and a woman raising a child doesn't mean they're going to do a better job of it. It's taken me a lot of soul searching and therapy to overcome some of the issues from my childhood traumas, so it simply comes down to parenting skills in order to raise a healthy bubba, and that's that.

So how do we deal with this stigma we face around having babies, raising our own families and becoming parents if we choose to? We crack on and do it regardless and let Karen cry about it all night long if she wants to. People will always have an opinion about who you are and the choices that you make, but you have one short life, so do what makes you happy. If you want to be a parent, that's your god-given right, and don't you let the homophobes stop you. I encourage you to do everything it takes in your pursuit of happiness. I'm a firm believer in what is meant for you will come to you, and you know me by now: if it means moving cities, cutting people off, changing jobs, I'm behind you, babes. I'm not going to pretend that having kids as a queer person is easy; it's no walk in the park. But that doesn't mean it's not possible.

When two women, or two people with ovaries, want to become a family, one of the hardest decisions they'll have to make is deciding which route to go down. From adoption and surrogacy to sperm donors and so on, it's an entire world for you to explore and to navigate. We know that for a lot of straight people, they can often fall pregnant by accident and it's common to hear them say, 'I didn't know I was ready to be a parent until it happened.' It's frustrating because on one hand, I don't believe you should have children unless you are absolutely desperate to, and another part of me is pissed because maybe I would want to be a parent if I just happened to fall pregnant with my partner. I'll never know because (hard as we sometimes try) my girlfriend is a cis woman and so can't impregnate me, and this is the first roadblock that lesbians often face with regards to parenthood. In our case, it's a conscious decision that we have to make, with financial and potentially emotional costs attached.

Meet Wegan...

We're Whitney and Megan Bacon-Evans, aka Wegan, and we both identify as she/her and use the label lesbian.

M: Ours is a rather unique love story as we met on Myspace! Whitney added me and I accepted, thinking she was a cute girl from Hawaii but that we'd never meet. Yet fast forward a year and Whitney came to study abroad in London in 2008. We met up the first weekend she arrived and in true lesbian fashion, two weeks later we were official!

Four years of long distance between the UK and Hawaii followed; we had her visa approved in 2012 and married in Palm Springs, California on 28 September 2017. We've been together for nearly fifteen years and still in love as ever and currently on our baby journey.

W: Early on in our relationship we both decided that we wanted children together and to become a family. We even had our future children's names picked out over a decade ago! We want to be able to expand our love and create amazing humans who we can be mothers to and to leave a legacy behind for our love story to continue for generations.

M: There's such a lack of representation and visibility around LGBTQ+ families. We asked our GP if we were entitled to any treatments on the NHS and they had no idea. [The NHS stands for the National Health Service, which provides health care for all UK citizens based on their need for medical care rather than their ability to pay for it.] We went down a rabbit hole and discovered not only barriers but ultimately discrimination in place. There were also so many decisions for us to make, how to find a sperm donor and who to carry first and what fertility treatments to opt for. There's a lot of big (and expensive) decisions to be made, which were overwhelming.

W: Initially we wanted to conceive via home insemination; however, were shocked to discover that this isn't actually possible. In 2005, the rules changed on sperm being sent to homes from sperm banks here in the UK, therefore we realized that we were being immediately forced into a clinical setting and would have to pay for everything privately. We decided we wanted to try to create awareness and change around the barriers and discrimination that exists against same-sex female couples. There is an unfair financial burden that is being placed on the LGBTQ+ community and the eligibility criteria in order to receive fertility treatment on the NHS.

M: We launched a petition in 2020 but unfortunately didn't receive the number of signatures required to create change. Not giving up, we decided to take legal action and launched a judicial review legal challenge against our local NHS health board (Frimley ICB) in October 2021 on the basis that the current IVF policy discriminated against lesbian couples. We did this in the hopes to set a precedent and be a catalyst for change for future LGBTQ+ families. In July 2022, we were delighted to see that the Government announced plans to fund fertility treatments for female same-sex couples in the Women's Health Strategy. If found to be successful, our case could positively impact the lives of tens of thousands, or even hundreds of thousands, of LGBTQ+ people embarking on their path to parenthood now and in the future to come.

W: Ignorant and insensitive questions like 'Who's the real mum?' or 'Who's the dad?' are still being thrown around in 2022. People often joke that lesbian couples should just 'Go find a bloke for a one-night stand,' and yet they'd never suggest that to a heterosexual couple that are struggling to conceive. Of course there's always the view that a child needs a mother and father as role models, which we all know not to be true. What is important is that our child grows up in a loving and supportive family. We often feel like lesbians are ignored but it's finally our time to shine!

Whitney Bacon-Evans and Megan Bacon-Evans

Let's face it, unless you're ready to have children, this family stuff might not be of interest to you. And if you are, you're going to do a whole lot more research than what I will provide you with in this chapter. There are some fantastic resources listed at the end of this book, and I highly recommend you follow Whitney and Megan Bacon-Evans on socials for some queer parent inspo. Thankfully in some parts of the world parenthood is something that we can actively think about as queer people and prepare for, should we want to. So whether you're educating yourself, are here to understand other points of view or are on the baby train yourself, here's what options you might have if you want to raise a family:

- IUI sperm donor insemination – Intrauterine insemination. A procedure where sperm is retrieved, usually from a sperm donor, and inserted by a doctor into the uterus of the person intending to carry.

- IVF sperm donor insemination – Similar to IUI, where donor sperm is used to impregnate an egg, but in IVF the eggs are removed from the body and fertilized in the lab. It entails taking hormone injections for approximately two weeks to produce eggs, then eggs are retrieved and fertilized with sperm before being transferred into the chosen person's uterus. Popularly, a lot of same-sex couples who both have ovaries choose to carry their partner's eggs so as to feel like it's a more shared experience. Of course one person in the relationship can do the whole shebang! Your family, your rules!

- IVF egg donor insemination – In some cases, there may be issues over the quality of a person's eggs, or some couples don't feel strongly about being genetically tied to their child but want to experience pregnancy. Whatever the reason, eggs can be donated from a friend or relative, but there are also donor egg banks, much like sperm banks.

- Surrogacy – A person who is not genetically related to the child agrees to carry a pregnancy for a couple or individual.

- Adoption – Domestic, international or foster care, adoption is the process of taking another person's child into one's custody, typically in a formal, legal way, in order to permanently act as their parent or guardian.

None of the above options come without cost – emotional, financial, and of course there are health risks associated with them, too. For example, IUI is a less invasive procedure on the body and involves fewer drugs than IVF, but in fact IVF offers higher success rates compared to IUI, and so there's plenty to weigh up. Whilst costs for these procedures vary according to country, state and so on, here in the UK, IUI costs between £350 and £1,600 per cycle at a private clinic, which in dollars is $400–$2,000. Of course most people who dream of being parents no doubt feel that bringing a baby into the world is a priceless experience, but those figures aren't to be sniffed at. Lower income households may find the costs involved to be insurmountable, or at the least overwhelming, making embarking on this journey to parenthood a tough one. Add to that the fact that the birthing industry isn't built to accommodate same-sex relationships in the way that it is for straight people, with gendered terminology and a general lack of support for the nonbiological parent, all adding up to make queer people less welcome in birthing services, unintentionally or not.

Fostering, adoption and surrogacy all have their hurdles too, and even just *thinking* about all of this can be a daunting process for couples wanting to embark on a parenting journey. But support is out there. Not just from your community and those who have parented before you, but from charities and organizations designed to guide and assist LGBTQ+ parents on this exciting path. If parenting is something that you choose to pursue, from all of the lesbian baby mamas I've spoken to the resounding chord is that patience and resilience are going to be key, both before and during parenthood. Parenting with a partner can be a testing time for the both of you. Lots of communication will be mandatory, remembering to value and cherish one another and having total nonjudgemental transparency, too. It's not just the impact of trying to parent as an LGBTQ+ person that you might face, but emotionally you may face feelings of body dysmorphia, of feeling othered as the nonbiological parent; you may experience postpartum depression or attachment anxiety through fostering – all of these things will add pressure to an already potentially stressful time. I say all of this to drive home the importance of being emotionally prepared because, let's face it, I'm only imagining how hard it must be. So times all of this by 1,000 and make your mental well-being your top priority. If you're a happy and healthy human inside of your brain, you're going to pass on those happy and healthy virtues to your child.

As I've been fairly certain for most of my adult life that babies are not my thing, I've always been straight up about it with those whom I've dated from the get go. I don't want to fall in love with someone who wants to make the two of us 'the three of us', because I know that would be the end of the relationship for me. It would be heartbreaking and such a waste of everybody's time to fall in love with someone who wants a life that looks nothing like the future you have envisioned for yourself. And no, you can't always help who you fall for, but you *can* be as open and honest about what you do want from the start. Like I've said, pregnancy isn't something that will just happen out of the blue for two women, and so it's always going to need a conversation one way or another. Depending on what age you are and what stage of life you're at, this is all relative, right? But the same rule is going to apply in any area of your life, at any age, and so open communication should always be a priority. Talking about how you feel, your wants and your needs is never going to be a detriment to your life; it will only ever improve it, significantly tbh. So long as you're being true to who you are, it's going to make your life much less complicated and much more fulfilling.

Mums are hot. Mums are so hot that you might find yourself falling for one and I sincerely hope that they're single, divorced or even widowed before you begin catching the feels (yes I've been there, done that and trust me you *don't want* the T-shirt). Being a potential step-parent can be super exciting, a wonderful addition to your life, but will no doubt be challenging. Blending a family takes a long time after all, five to seven years on average, and there are so many different types of blended families that you could be stepping into.[9] Your new boo may have been in a heterosexual relationship before you came along and next thing you know you're the big lesbian gatecrasher who no one invited. Fun! You might be mum's new gal pal who just happens to be there when they wake up *and* when they go to sleep. A whole myriad of options awaits you, but being prepared for being in a relationship with little humans who, rightly, come first has its own battles. You have to put your ego aside for one thing, or be prepared for the ex, the other parent, to always be around. Nobody said life is easy, and with the twenty-first century giving us more freedom than ever, it means there are some seriously complex family situations out there. Not everyone is built to navigate those and so understanding yourself, your boundaries and what is important to you is really key. It's commitment from the beginning. There are no flings when kids are involved, but the rewards can feel far sweeter for being harder won.

You might be the hot mum who's already got a family and is either newly single, questioning your sexuality or even discovering your queerness. Realizing or acting on your sexuality a little later in life, or after you've had children, is a whirlwind of a thing, but it's also bloody exciting! First, welcome to the community! You are so loved and valued here and I'm so proud of your bravery and openness. Don't let others' perceptions stand in your way now that you're here. Friends, family, your kids and your ex-partner will all have their own thoughts, vocal or not, but it's your life and only you know how you feel and what's right for you. You might hear things like, 'You're going through a phase,' or, 'You're just having a midlife crisis.' You might have your new feelings simplified, mocked or even disapproved of, but babe, you know in your gut who you are, and the only approval you need is your own. Make sure to mentally take time out for you. There's a whole self-love chapter coming your way and I want you to really invest in it. I know plenty of women who have had this realization and their entire lives, friendships, hobbies, even books and media they've consumed have been built around heterosexuality and so are upended. Reaching out, talking to and finding new friends is no bad thing. It's not always easy, starting again, but it's nothing to be ashamed of and it is so worth it if this is your true path. Living authentically is the most important thing in the world and once you're there you simply can't turn back. You deserve to be happy and to be loved and there are a shit tonne of lesbians out here waiting to meet someone just like you. So go get 'em.

Meet Natalie...

I'm Natalie Lee, my pronouns are she/her and I identify as pansexual or bisexual, I don't really mind.

Thinking back, maybe I'd always been attracted to women but had dismissed it because being heterosexual was the only option on the table. I remember having this very fleeting but equally puzzling and exhilarating feeling when I was a teen working in a clothes store. A woman with long, brown hair waltzed in confidently, throwing clothes at me as I assisted her in the changing room. I was transfixed. I remember having a very physical reaction to her and didn't understand whether I wanted to be her, make love to her or make her my best friend. So, I put it to the back of my mind and carried on doing what was accepted and expected: chasing boys. I wonder how different my life would have been if I had had the knowledge, understanding and language to explore those feelings. Would I be a divorced mother of two right now? Who knows.

Despite my feminist protestations, I loved being cared for by a man. I liked them paying for meals out, mowing the lawn and running downstairs with a baseball bat if we heard a noise in the middle of the night. I felt protected and safe. And that was important to me after growing up in a sometimes-volatile environment. Occasionally I'd daydream about being with a woman, wondering what it felt like to be in a relationship with the same sex. Wondering whether the softness of her skin would feel odd and who would sort out the household bills or put up the flat-pack bunk bed. I don't remember thinking it was a viable option until after my separation and subsequent divorce.

What I now know from having a relationship with a woman is that it felt glorious; it felt warm and cosy yet bubbly and exciting. It felt like coming home. More natural and normal than I had even dared to dream. The softness was incredible and I couldn't believe I'd been missing out on this feeling until my forties.

What was challenging was unpacking all the bullshit, the happily ever after fairy tales. I had to do a lot of soul searching and I had to finally understand who I was. I had to acknowledge that much of my decision-making had been about childhood wounds. I had to heal myself, and my exploration of my sexuality led to a deeper awakening about who I was and how society has shaped me. And even though I'm single now, I feel free enough to explore and am excited about this new phase of my life.

I believe the most valuable thing we can do for our children, for everyone, is to not assume heterosexuality. It's not our decision to make, it's not the default. Let's give everyone the option to explore and have adventures with whoever they choose to. Let's not condemn and judge them for taking ownership of their story. Let's communicate honestly and openly. Not everyone's happy ending looks the same, and that's okay.

Let's enable people to be free to love and have consensual sex with whoever they want to. Let's make sure sex education focuses on inclusion rather than excluding a large majority of the population from its very white, heteronormative lens. Most of all, let's give everyone the right to be whoever they want to be without eye rolls, whispered gossip, forced announcements, outright discrimination, threats of violence and more – as long as it's not causing harm to others, why are we so bothered about who people decide to love? Let's allow people to be themselves even if that makes you feel uncomfortable for a moment or two.

Natalie Lee

You could be like me, skim reading this chapter and yawning, lowering your five-star review of this book to a four-point-five because this chapter hasn't given you anything to think about (gimme a sec to change your mind!). You're too young to be thinking about this maybe, or you already know you don't want kids. Well, remember my engagement to Chloe? A year in, I was driving to work one day, in the throes of love for her and pictured a little blonde baby. A chubby little thing all giggling and bouncing away in my arms, and I couldn't believe it. A hint of maternalism? Chloe wanted a family, and I wanted her. So the more I looked to our future, I had no choice but to have them appear in my projections. Life is a series of sliding doors. Different decisions you make that lead to such different outcomes. I would have had babies with her, but we wouldn't have been happy because ultimately, that isn't what I want for my life. It would have been one of the most selfish things that I could have done, to put her wants and needs above my own. I'd have been stuck doing school runs when what I really want is to be travelling the coast of Italy with the roof down and no real plan of where I'm going next. I learned from that experience and have never made the same mistake again.

You can get lost in people, in relationships. You can get swept up in romance and make decisions that you wish you could change when your head is no longer in the clouds. And so you have to be sure to take responsibility for yourself, always. Of course it's wonderful to get caught up in the moment, to throw caution to the wind and to act spontaneously once in a while. Just make sure that whatever decisions you make are for the long run, with all possible outcomes in mind. Of course you'll make mistakes, hell, we all do! But it's all about learning from them and growing from them, in order to be the happiest version of you. Make a mistake once, you don't do it again, and if you do, get your ass in therapy. I know who I am now and what I want is clearer than ever. I want to dote on my nieces and nephews, and my friends' babies, but in the end I want a life with my partner without the restrictions or responsibilities of kids. That's just me.

Following accounts that share their journey to parenthood is such a useful place to begin if you're thinking about babies, are unsure, or simply want to learn more. Thankfully there are lots of wonderfully open and informative accounts across socials who are letting us in on their lives and follow along step by step. It's comforting to see people similar to you who are on that path and who are giving you an unfiltered idea of just what parenthood really involves. I beg you not to pay heed to the 'beige mums'. The ones who seem like they have it all together online in their perfectly beige homes with their perfectly unspoilt soft furnishings. Bleugh! Head for the honest mamas, the ones who don't mind telling you that their child has been a little shit at nursery today, or that they miss nappy-free date nights. Because I guess that's what life is really going to look like! I'd also suggest seeking out charities or trusts who specialize in support for whatever road you decide to go down. Whether it's with a donor, adoption or foster care, finding a trusted centre of support is going to be so useful in this process.

Leaning on your friends and family for support, being open about this chapter of your life, is possibly something to also consider. A healthy support network can be a real lifesaver when it comes to raising a family, if not just to have a few babysitters on hand for the super tough days. There's also the very real possibility of fertility issues to think about. Trigger warning here – miscarriage, for example, is extremely common and sadly is still a taboo or unspoken topic, which makes sharing pregnancy struggles tough for a lot of people. So again, this is where that trusted and kind support network is important. I know that being vulnerable, whilst it can be scary, is such a powerful way to connect with other humans, and in doing so creates an incredibly strong bond of support.

And speaking of vulnerability, most of us have health check-ups to make sure our bodies are doing okay, so why not do the same thing for your brain? Sitting down with your partner and talking to a therapist to make sure your heads are in the right place, that you've both really thought through this shared journey together, could be a really useful thing to do. It could be used to iron out any concerns, make sure you're both ready for this life-changing experience and to have really talked through the ins and outs of what's potentially to come. We're taking the time to really check in with ourselves on a deeper level before making any life-changing decisions, because we're badass, smart lesbians. Our aim is to live intentionally, and I'm about to talk you through some of my tried and tested ways of doing so in the next chapter.

Recently, here in the UK, there has been an incredible step forward for queer couples, who are now able to receive IVF treatment on the NHS, something straight people have been eligible for since the early eighties. Whilst we can often feel like the road to equality is never ending, these small steps forward should be celebrated, because a more equal world *is* possible if we continue to advocate and show up and demand our human rights. It's not your job to be an activist should you choose to parent; no LGBTQ+ person should be made to do that. But you will be advocating for the community just by being yourself. By showing up to a clinic with your partner, going to parents' evenings unabashedly or by teaching your child that love is not bound by gender for them to pass onto the world in their own way. You deserve to parent. Queer families are important. Quite frankly, I think if we were given the task of raising the world, it would be a far better place for it.

Chapter 11

The Art of Intentional Living

ositive vibes only! Live with no regrets! Stop living in the past! Live, laugh, love!

We've all heard people talking like this, seen posts like this on socials, and I'm here to tell you that all of the above needs to be put in a box and buried forever, because toxic positivity culture is literally killing people. Live, Laugh, *Lesbian*, on the other hand, is here to save you! And look, if you know me and follow me on socials, you might be thinking, erm? Helen? Positivity queen? Have you fallen over and knocked your little blonde head? I know, I admit, it might seem like I'm being a total hypocrite. But there's a difference between being faux positive, covering your ears and not acknowledging sadness or emotional depth and actually just having a naturally positive disposition. I'm the latter, if you couldn't tell.

I've not written this book to simply talk about myself and my own life and to just give you some affirmations to say in the mirror. Do I believe in positive affirmations? Hell yeah! But what actually happened to me when I tried that approach without looking at and adapting other areas of my life too, is that I ended up quite severely depressed. After years of going through cycles of compassion fatigue (we'll talk about that in Chapter 12), I ended up in some very dark places, feeling terribly alone and defeated and confused by life. It doesn't work, babe. Tricking your brain into thinking positively without doing the deeper work isn't going to lead to a happy ending, a grand finale or what we're aiming for: a fulfilled life. Luckily, I've tried a shit tonne of other ways to become the happiest version of me, not just in my sexuality but in my overall self, in being the very best Helen I can be. Now it's your turn.

Over the last twenty-nine days I've quit smoking, written a huge chunk of this book, gone sober whilst I write and also deleted all of the food delivery apps from my phone. An overhaul, if you will. And honestly, I didn't mean to do all of these things at once, and tbh, I wouldn't recommend it because it's been a hell of a ride. I tell you this not to brag, but to say that evolving into a better version of you can happen at any age, at any time, and can happen over and over again throughout your life. There's no divine timing to reaching your happiest self because it's a conscious choice you're going to have to make over and over again. Sounds daunting and a bit laborious maybe, but isn't that a gift to have the opportunity, whenever you want to, to just invest a little more in yourself?

I'm gonna sound like a boring old fart here – they don't call me your lesbian big sister for nothing – but learning the art of looking after yourself is the very first step to being your happiest self. Self-love is really *one* thing. God, I feel like Oprah or one of those Instagram gurus here, but I swear this is one thing that I know to be absolutely true (other than the fact that lesbians rule): it's having respect for yourself. Self-love is simply having respect for yourself. Respecting your good, your bad, your flaws and imperfections. It's taking the time to look after yourself, to get to know yourself better, forgive your mistakes and behaviours of the past and to strive to be better for no one other than yourself. Respecting yourself makes way for self-love, self-worth, and your confidence and self-esteem to soar. Once you really respect *you*, everything else can begin to slot into place. It's the very foundation of self-love and self-care, and so using that thought as a starting point is the very best thing that you can do.

Self-respect means honouring your worth, which sounds downright woo woo, I know, but I'm a very straight-talking kinda gal, and it's true. When you can be proud of who you are, of your abilities and traits, when you know that you're worthy of love, of kindness and happiness, that's when life gets really bloody exciting. It's the most freeing feeling you'll experience and is the exact place I wish all humans were able to live from. First, you have to accept and believe that you're worthy of looking after yourself. Consciously or subconsciously, your sexuality has a huge effect on your self-respect because of everything you've been taught about the LGBTQ+ community. If you were taught or have taken on negative connotations about queer people, knowing your sexuality will make you feel inherently bad, whether you realize it or not. This is where you need to take hold of your self-respect, to make sure that you're important in your own eyes and to take responsibility for your actions against yourself. Self-respect is vital because it impacts *every* area of your life.

I smoked for almost twenty years. Much like alcoholism or drug use, nicotine in cigarettes is a drug and I was addicted to it. But it wasn't the addiction that kept me smoking; it was my acceptance of who I was. I *believed* myself to be a smoker, that it was part of my identity, and I forgave myself for inhaling smoke into my lungs time and time again. Now, I'm a smart girl, I'm an A* student to be frank, and what finally made me quit was that I realized that I was being ignorant to my own behaviours. I was pushing the knowledge that what I was doing was killing me to the back of my head. I was treating myself like I'm stupid. I was disrespecting myself over and over again by actively doing something that I know is bad for me. Now there is no room for self-respect when you're doing that to yourself day in, day out. And honestly, I've considered myself to be in love with me for some years now, but I truly just took things to a whole new level.

It's been twenty-nine days and my self-respect has gone through the roof. I won't lie, I feel pretty smug. I feel very pro-Helen, pro-health, pro-living life to the full, pro-change, pro-self-respect. And fuck, I love myself for it! This is just one aspect of my life where I realized I was deeply disrespecting myself, and it's come after the soul-searching years of my twenties when everyone thinks you should have everything figured out. But like I've said, and I want you to remind yourself, you're ever evolving, ever changing, and it's about going with that flow and growing with yourself. Smoking is one example of that, but over the years there have been many things I've realized were disrespectful to myself in my search for self-love and fulfilment.

I'm talking about smoking when this book is clearly about your sexuality. I know it might seem a bit off topic, but everything matters when it comes to loving yourself. If I want you to quit anything, it would be hating on yourself, but you have to feel like you're worthy of being loved in the first place and it's all the small things that will help you to get there. You might be thinking as you're reading this, 'Okay, so to reach fulfilment and happiness I have to respect myself. I have to believe I'm worthy of love and I have to look at myself in the mirror and really like who I am. But what if I don't like the fact that I'm gay? What if I wish I was born different, Helen? How do I come to terms with who I am then?'

The first thing to remember is that if you're not happy with your sexuality, it's not because *you* don't like yourself. I know that might sound a bit backwards, but it's not you who taught yourself that being queer is wrong, or different, or bad. Those aren't your actual opinions. You've picked up and absorbed all of these connotations about sexuality from others around you, and so the problem isn't even about your queerness, it's that you're judging yourself. Let that sink in for a moment. You don't hate your sexuality, you're just full of self-judgement because of what others think, and this isn't actually a *you* problem, babe. We now have to help your brain get to grips with this information and to create more positive thoughts and feelings around your identity. If you're here and not hating your sexuality, this exercise we're about to do can work for any problem you might face. Body image, self-esteem, a work problem or life issue. Regardless, let's learn some skills to help improve our well-being from the inside out.

Let's start by making a list of all of the negative thoughts or problems that you're feeling. Put them down in order of severity, and then we're going to write a remedy or solution for each of them. This might take some time and effort depending on how easy it is for you to articulate your thoughts, so light some candles, put on some soothing music, give yourself plenty of time and let's get into it. Remember, no one has to see this, and so be brutally honest in order to really do something about the way that you're feeling. Here are some examples:

- I feel alone, like I'm different to those around me.

    Remedy: I can invest some time and effort into meeting other queer people who love who they are. I could join an LGBTQ+-focused group or club to surround myself with similar people. I can put myself out there to make one good LGBTQ+ friend, but also to make one really good straight friend who's an ally to the community and supports me.

- I feel very insecure and don't value who I am.

    Remedy: I'm going to find and invest in one thing that I'm good at and seek out other people who do something similar so we can talk about our shared passion. I'll share my feelings with someone who loves me to better understand where my feelings are coming from, and I will make friends with somebody who can act as a role model or mentor to aspire to.

- I have religious guilt about my sexuality.

    Remedy: I could read a book on modern faith, find articles on gay tolerance and seek out positive literature around LGBTQ+ faith. I could find a queer friend who has the same faith as I do and also seek out a queer pastor for guidance and support.

Once you've identified the areas that are impacting you the most, you can begin to form less self-destructive beliefs about being queer. Actively work on remedying these negative feelings every single day because no one is going to come along and save you from yourself. I wish I could take these thoughts away for you; I wish you never had to have these horrid assumptions about your sexuality in the first place.

But you can't change the past, you can only take a hold of your future and decide what you're going to feel about yourself from here on out. You are a beautiful, unique person with unique value in this world. This is who you are, and a lot depends on confronting the challenge of loving yourself head-on with a positive outcome in mind.

Other disruptive thoughts or actions that impact your low level of self-respect are:

- You say negative things and are critical about yourself.

- You can't seem to say 'No'.

- You compare yourself to others and think of yourself negatively afterwards.

- You're there for everyone else but no one seems to be there for you.

- You struggle to speak up for yourself.

- You feel incompetent, unloved or inadequate.

If any of this is sounding like you (and look, we're all human and so these things are bound to creep into our minds from time to time) or if this is common for you, then it's time for a shake-up. I know from experience that feeling any of these things is *exhausting*. It's utterly debilitating hating on yourself all of the time. There are often cycles with it, contributing factors like food, drugs and relationships, and so it's a lot to contend with if you're trying to take hold of your own mind once and for all. But you can do it; I absolutely know that you can.

First things first, let's get mindful of our thoughts, of our actions, and the choices that we make. Being mindful starts to make us aware and to really think about what we're doing and how we're acting. Take my smoking, for example: as soon as I became mindful about it, I immediately stopped and now I can't ever go back, because I'm really thinking about what I'm doing and it makes no sense to continue. To get into that headspace, you have to first slow down. Stop living on fast forward and really force yourself to be present, and think about what's happening in the very moment you're living in. Once you've slowed the brain and mind down, you can start to really understand what you're thinking about and notice the ways in which you talk to yourself and make decisions. A lot of people do this in the form of meditation, or journaling, or talking to themselves in the mirror whilst brushing their teeth in the morning. To get into the habit, giving yourself a daily ritual where you dedicate a moment of time to being mindful is a great start, otherwise it ends up being like the vitamins you bought that now sit forgotten at the back of the cupboard behind the baked beans. Having a focused portion of time, daily, to be mindful is a great place to begin.

During that mindful time, we're looking to be nonjudgemental about ourselves, about the things that we think and feel, and to be patient whilst we learn this new skill and habit. The aim is to start to understand ourselves better and to accept ourselves for who we are, to be loving and kind towards ourselves and to let go of things that no longer serve us or make us feel good, or past actions that we may not be proud of. Getting real personal with who you are and letting go of the idea that we need to please others, or that we need to be liked by everybody. Someone said to me once, 'You don't like everybody, so why do you expect everybody to like you?' It's so true! And it's about time we accept that about life: particularly because of our sexuality, there are gonna be haters, but what really matters is whether *you* love you. You deserve to, so get practising.

When embarking on this journey to being more confident in who we are, loving ourselves and changing some bad habits, it can sometimes feel a little lonely, and this is where having a supportive network around you is really important. It's time to start setting boundaries with people around you who may have become very comfortable with the old you. The you who wasn't this self-loving, confident and self-respecting person. And that may take some getting used to. It may even take some letting go of certain people, even family members, and that's not always easy. I spent ten years in a friendship that was really all about what that person could get from me, and it wasn't until I reached my thirties that I finally said to myself, 'Enough is enough.' It was as simple as unfriending them across all socials and deleting their number from my phone, but the psychological strength to do that was the hardest part. Having the self-respect to say, 'no more' and to stick to it. No dramas, no cross words, just no more. There's always time in life to make new friends, to connect with new people who are on your wavelength and who are as self-respecting as the new you is. Your tribe, as we know, is changeable and can evolve with you throughout your life, so start to recognize the types of people who are good to be around and head towards the healthy and positive relationships that make you and your inner mind feel good.

Setting some healthy boundaries around the time you spend on socials is another great thing to do. I love socials; I'm part of an entire community online and it brings me so much joy in so many ways. From fashion inspo to global news to friendships, I would never have made it without it.

It's a wonderful place to be, but we all know that there are downsides to the online world, too. It's so easy to compare yourself to others online: their appearance, their lifestyle, their apparent happiness and success. We all know that what we see online isn't a full representation of other people's lives, but in the moment it's so easy to forget. Take some healthy time off socials now and again to practise being present, to practise gratitude and to really engage in real life. That's the time that you're going to remember when you're old and grey anyhow. The things that you did and experienced in life, the friendships you made and the trips you took, not the hours you wasted scrolling online. According to a recent study published in the journal *Cyberpsychology, Behavior and Social Networking*, a social media break of just a week can reduce anxiety and depression.[10] Getting offline on a regular basis has had one of the most positive impacts on my mental health that I've experienced.

I did a one-to-one mentoring session with someone recently who was looking to improve their confidence in public speaking, and after an hour in her presence I knew that it wasn't her presenting skills that needed work, it was her self-confidence. It was simply the little voice in her ear questioning herself constantly, bringing up imposter-like feelings and making her doubt her capabilities. You know the voice I'm talking about, right? And if we could all switch that voice off inside our heads, gosh, there'd be no stopping us! The more you practise that mindfulness, the more you'll start to notice just how often that voice pops up and just how spiteful it can be. When you hear it, take back control of your own mind and say the following phrase out loud if you can: 'I don't speak to myself or anyone else that way,' and carry on with what you were doing. You can even go one step further and turn that thought around into something positive. Say things like, 'I am good at this,' 'I am beautiful,' 'I deserve this,' 'I am an incredible friend.' Using positive self-affirmations to build your self-esteem isn't woo woo, babes, it's taking control of your mind, the most powerful thing you own, and changing your life for the better.

Not all of us have a super active imagination, can picture things clearly in our minds or find it easy to acutely decipher what we think and feel. Some of us will feel a bit muddy in the brain, or as though our minds are working too fast to fully comprehend what we're thinking, or we may have a sense of blankness, numbness even. These practices can be especially tricky for those of us with ADHD, who are neuro-divergent, who are autistic or have bipolar disorder. So many things can impact how we use our brains, and for any of us, none of what I'm telling you to do is *easy*, I know that. But you *can* do this. It might need tweaking – we're all different – just be sure to find what works for you and do it. Make a list and read it often. Stick Post-It notes around your home. Set reminders on your phone to sporadically give yourself a compliment. Whatever it takes, it should be your absolute top priority to build that inner sense of respect, confidence and love for yourself, and just watch how you blossom.

Meet Shantania...

I'm Shantania, my pronouns are she/her and I just flow. I don't really like to identify as anything; I just do what I feel and I don't conform to what society says I should do. As long as it doesn't hurt anybody, as long as I'm happy and the other person's happy, I'm good.

From when I was young, I always thought everybody had similar thoughts going on in their head. I feel like it's not that we're all so different, it's just that some people act on their impulses and some choose not to. Especially when it comes to girls, I feel like we're so loving, we're so feminine and we're able to appreciate each other differently. When I was in school I would always like the prettiest girl that all the boys liked and then I'd end up being her friend because I thought she was just so amazing. I had two wives in grade four! I would be like their protector.

Jamaica back in the day was full of homophobia. On the taxis people would write 'burn chi chi man', which is 'burn gay men'. Shaming gay culture was a real thing and there was such negativity around it. For me, I don't respond to negative older people, I just find them really weird. I don't have time to sit there for them to lecture me. I'm dreamy but I'm a realist and I can see what's happening around me and what's going on with people. I could always see that everybody has their thoughts and some act on them, some don't, some run away. It's natural!

When I moved to the UK I saw lots of different gay people and I was really intrigued. I wanted to make friends with them because I thought they seemed so cool and interesting and showed loads of love, and I like the differences in people. Being here I can do what I want in a sense without having crazy repercussions, but I wouldn't be able to do the same things if I was back in Jamaica. I would be a bit more nervous to be myself, and it's not our fault, it's just how society is set up there.

Back in Jamaica I'm seen as a role model in all aspects of life. Everything that I've been through from being homeless to being in an interracial relationship to being with a girl, all of that is showing people that you can live your life how it suits you and you're gonna grow from it regardless. I want to inspire people with whatever I do because it gives them more hope. Of course we all live in different countries so there's certain ways you have to move in different environments to make sure that you're safe.

My mum is a traditional Rastafarian woman, right? So being gay is against the belief system, but at the same time she loves LGBTQ+ people! She watches all of my friends on social media but she doesn't want it for me. She wants me to be with a man and to have kids and that's it. And I do get that. But I said to her, 'There's a part of my life where I have to experience it and I have no regrets, I'm happy and I love women.' I don't want to be my mum in that sense, I want to be me with my own thoughts and it's gotten me far. I feel like she needs to just catch up a bit. She has no choice but to accept me, which I know can come across as rude, but I pay the bills, I take care of myself and her, so let me live my life.

It takes a lot to find true peace and to feel happy. Work hard, stack your paper and move if you need to. You've got one life on this earth and you can't just sit there in this space being miserable for the rest of it. That's not what you were born to do. A lot of people have made it in different countries and different places on their own, me being one of them. If there's a will, there's a way, and if there are still countries and cities where you can hustle or work hard and be accepted rather than stay somewhere where your whole core is being stifled, go save yourself. Save your mind first, and the rest will follow.

Shantania Beckford

Less brain stuff, more actionable remedies to self-love now. And yes, I'm going to be that basic bitch and talk about the three things you'll have heard over and over again, but 'if it ain't broke, don't fix it', so here goes. Sleep, water and exercise. Outside of your mindfulness, these are going to be the biggest game changers to your overall health and well-being. I can't stress to you enough the huge impact that not getting these three things does to your mood, your ability to self-care and ultimately to be happy. Dehydration depletes the levels of amino acids in your brain, leading to feelings of anxiety, irritability and inadequacy. Drink the bloody water, I beg you! If you're having problems sleeping, you might be more likely to feel anxious, depressed or even suicidal. Lavender oil, soothing sleep sounds, get off your damn phone and close your eyes, whatever it takes: invest in getting the best possible sleep that you can. And lastly, research shows that people who exercise regularly have better mental health and emotional well-being and lower rates of mental illness.[11] Walk, gym, take up a sport, do whatever it takes to get moving. And look, I know going for a walk doesn't cure depression, but it's certainly not going to make you feel worse, so it's worth applying yourself to it for a period of time and tracking the results, right? Sadly, there's no one quick fix to alleviate negative emotions, but a combination of self-respecting steps can certainly help us to get to a place where we can better deal with what's going on inside of us.

Another actionable step that you can take on the journey to self-love is giving back. Not necessarily in a financial way, but when you do things for others, it can give you a great sense of selflessness that could change how you feel about yourself entirely. Taking the spotlight off of yourself and shining some light on others gives your mind room to value what's really important and could well open up a little nook in that brain for self-love to drip feed in. Volunteering is an option, and charities are always in need of extra hands. Offering help to those in need can be a really rewarding experience that shows you that true value lies outside of your sexual identity, and more in your kindness of heart.

You're probably thinking, 'Wow, we're almost at the end of the chapter and she hasn't mentioned the T word!' Psych! Here it comes, babes. Therapy! Oh wonderful, therapy. Hella expensive, yes, but if you pay for a gym membership to look after your body, why aren't you paying a therapist to help look after your brain? Your mind is the most powerful muscle in your entire body and controls every decision and movement that you make. Learning how to use it and strengthen it is surely one of life's greatest investments. There are so many different forms of therapy. It's not accessible to everyone and doesn't work for everyone either, but if it is an option for you, then it's well worth a good hunt and a touch of perseverance to find the right kind of therapy or therapist for you.

For years, I didn't realize that my romantic relationships were failing because of childhood trauma. I thought my brain was just broken and that I was innately bad. It was really damaging to my self-esteem because I didn't realize that I was acting off of impulses derived from learned behaviours in my childhood. Things like cheating on partners, picking fights when things were going well and blowing up relationships because I didn't know what calm, happy and safe love looked like. I sought therapy in my late twenties, at my wits' end with myself, and learned that all of these behaviours weren't because I was an asshole after all! I learned that we don't do things without reason (unless we're psychopaths), and that whilst I'd learned and picked up some pretty shit psychological beliefs that led to me making terrible decisions at times, I could unlearn them and activate new ones to lead a happier life.

Now, I'm not going to say that therapy fixes you, but it attempts to help you to change thought patterns that lead to unhappiness, and to learn emotional-regulation skills that help you to live your life in a more positive way. This all sounds very deep and serious, but at the very least, therapy gives you an outlet to say exactly how you think and feel to someone who isn't judging you and is professionally adept at helping you overcome your problems. It's one of the best investments I ever made and is definitely something you should look into if you have the means to do so. You can find a bunch of different links and suggestions in the back of the book.

We're constantly inundated with adverts and media that are telling us how we should live, how we should look, think or feel, and quite frankly, it's a head fuck. It's no wonder we question who we are or experience feelings of unworthiness. So learning the art of intentional living, which is what all of the above is helping you to do, allows you to take a step back and to refocus on what really matters to you, to take back control of your life. Although there are systemic issues all over the world that lead to negative bias about the LGBTQ+ community, we have to focus on what we can first change, which is ourselves. We have to take the personal initiative to figure out how we can live a more intentional and emotionally healthy life today, so that we can continue to create change for tomorrow. For our happily ever after, if there is such a thing.

Undisputedly you are important, you are worthy, you are fucking phenomenal to be totally honest with you, and you deserve to know and to feel that about yourself. If in doubt, Famalam, always remember this: if you need someone to believe in you, I do.

Chapter 12

Happily Ever After

Humans are incredibly multifaceted, and just one of our facets is our sexuality. Because we're a minority in our sexual identity, being a lesbian or a queer person can often feel all-consuming and as though it's a ruling factor in our lives. For me, it is a ruling factor and I love it that way. It's very much a part of my everyday life to speak about sexuality and to encourage others to thrive in their queer skin. I'm someone who works in the field that I'm in, showcasing my personality and life for the world to see, but I know that of course it's not that way for everyone. And I understand that when a part of you is outside of the heteronormative narrative, it can feel like there are constant battles to fight and opinions and laws to contend with when all you want to do is, well, be you! Our queerness and our experience of it is unique to all of us, but for those of us waiting for the clouds to part, the sun to shine in and for life to start looking positively rosy on the regular, I've got to be honest and tell you something. Happily ever afters don't exist. I know! I'm a cow for leaving that part until the very end, but I'm sorry to break it to you, babes, life just doesn't work that way.

If you were waiting until the final chapter for that one magic sentence that would change your life overnight, I'm afraid I've got to disappoint you. Although there are some absolutely cracking quotes throughout this book that I'm sure do just that. But sadly, 'happily ever after' is a damn trope. An overused plot or storyline in movies and books to sell us the dream that things, people or lifestyles can save us, because that's far more romantic than us pulling on our own pair of big girl pants and saving ourselves. Happily ever after teaches us that the forces of evil can be defeated, whether that be wicked witches or, in our case, homophobia, and even better that the conflict will end with a happy marriage to the man (ahem, woman) of your dreams. The truth is, you can live contentedly, but it's got nothing to do with being rescued by a handsome princess (although we wouldn't say no), but rather starts and ends with you, and finding your own kind of happy.

Happiness isn't an end goal; it's not a target to reach nor a tangible thing to possess. There's no finite moment and it isn't a state that you find yourself in and then, poof, you stay there forever. But that doesn't mean that you can't find a consistent pattern of satisfaction and gratitude in your life that gives you the same sense of calm and steadiness that happiness does. Seeking out and learning about what makes you tick, what brings you joy and what works best in order for you to maintain that state of mind is what we're aiming for. Contentment, for example, is just as rewarding as happiness and is possibly a more accurate concept to aim for. I think if we look at happiness objectively, it's not actually a feeling but rather a continued mark of things like joy and elation, and is, when you really think about it, almost temporary, attached to moments and material things. Contentment, on the other hand, is a long-lasting sense of peacefulness, gratitude and satisfaction. It feels like a hot bath swaddling your limbs and making you feel safe. The best part is that there's no limitation on the amount of contentment that you can experience, which leads to a very happy state, indeed. And that's what we've been working towards throughout this book. You don't have to be overjoyed every day; you don't have to beam from ear to ear and skip down the street in order for life to be a sweet one. Contentment in who you are is only going to aid your sense of happiness in the long run.

My therapist introduced me to something called compassion fatigue. I discovered the power of The Secret in my mid-twenties, the idea that thoughts and energy attract what you think about, how thoughts become things and how the words you say in your mind appear in your reality. So came my era of toxic positivity. I refused to let myself feel anything other than 'good thoughts' and 'positive thoughts', from not being pissed off when I missed my train to forgiving people for bad things they'd done. I trained my brain to only ever be 'happy', and of course, that little world I'd created came crumbling down very quickly. I crashed hard, and for two weeks I had what I thought was burnout, where I couldn't move, couldn't hold a conversation, I just slept, cried and sat in numbness and had no idea what was happening to me. This cycle happened again and again over the next few years. A few months would go by and I'd be so happy and positive and on a high constantly, then crash hard for a week or two and not have any explanation for it. My therapist explained to me that compassion fatigue is described as the negative cost of caring, that because I was trying to put out so much positivity and empathy and #goodvibes, it was leading to utter exhaustion.

See, we're not designed to be happy all of the time; on a basic evolutionary level, our brains just aren't built that way. We live in a world where we thrive on extrinsic rewards. Things that we can buy and attain super easily like a coffee en route to work, or a new pair of trainers all the way through to a new car, house or designer purchase (show me the Chanel!). Each time we 'reward ourselves' our brains get a glorious hit of dopamine, and the problem is that over time, we need more and more 'things' to reach that same high. Intrinsic motivation, on the other hand, gives us a much more long-lasting sense of pleasure. Things like painting for the sake of it or playing football on a Sunday because you love to play. Despite bringing an intangible sense of joy, with less instant gratification attached to it, or more of a drip feed as opposed to a rush of dopamine, these things are much more aligned with the long-term contentment that I'm encouraging you to seek.

Why am I banging on about all this? Well, whilst we may be looking for quick fixes in the way that we feel about our sexuality or our identity and about ourselves, I think what life teaches us about anything is that it's very much a journey with no shortcuts. You've got to strap yourself in for the ride, and those who really throw themselves into it are the ones who seem to have the most interesting stories to tell. Just as there's no thing that you can buy that will make you happy forever, there's no book you can read to change your life overnight. It's for you to figure out your 'happy', and it's people like me who you can lean on along the way.

I hope that you can see by now just how wonderful you

are. How being you is perfectly normal, perfectly fantastic, and I wonder if you know just how rare it is for you to even be alive today. The odds of your parents meeting are 1 in 20,000. Multiply that by the chances of them staying together long enough to have kids, that's 1 in 2,000, and so the actual probability of you existing, *at all*, comes out to 1 in $10^{2,685,000}$. Yes. That's a 10 followed by 2,685,000 zeroes! Isn't it an incredible, spectacular thing that you're even here, gracing us with your presence in the first place? Blessing us with your being, with your unique thoughts and feelings and your contributions to the world? So don't tell me that you aren't worthy, because you're more than worthy. You're a freaking miracle, okay?

So you've accepted that you're a miracle, that it's no mistake that you've ended up on this earth thinking and feeling exactly as you do, and that from coming out to having babies, it's really about taking the reins of your life to end up leading a fulfilled one. It's deciding not to listen to what you may have been taught, and to instead trust and lean into who you are, unapologetically. And in order to help you and support you in doing that, you should surround yourself with people who love you, who can relate to you and build you up whenever you need it. It's always your decision how, when and where to come out, if at all, and you can label yourself however you bloody like. That also doesn't have to be set in stone if you no longer feel as though the lesbian shoe fits. Choose wisely when it comes to love, be free with your exploration of your sexuality and of course, communicate like a MF. I'll keep reminding you until I'm blue in the face: it's the power of communication that's going to be one of the best skills you can build on and master throughout your life, gay or not! And lastly, there are a tonne of queer humans out here waiting to fall in love with someone just like you, because you're magic.

I'd be lying if I said to you that I wake up every day and instantly think about how grateful I am to live in my skin. I mainly think about coffee, first, and then I look over at my girlfriend and try to stop myself from squishing her face 'cause she's so cute (she's a grouch if I wake her up too early). I might then do a mental run-down of my day, and then I get up and I live my life. However, there are moments every day where I force myself to stop and action the mindfulness that we talked about in the previous chapter, and I think to myself, 'Thank god I'm not straight!' Not to offend the hettys, but I really am so grateful to have a queer perspective of the world, to love more freely than most, to be as open and accepting and loving as I am, and I hope that by now you can see all of those wonderful attributes in yourself, too. Because you deserve to love yourself wholeheartedly, and I would fill you up with that knowledge like a wonderful vase full of flowers if I could. Wouldn't it be a sad life to live in ignorance or judgement? And I know I have the privilege to think that way because of the society that I live in. I've talked about how if you're able to be out like I am, you're far luckier than most. But with the power of community and of us standing together and pushing forward as one, we can dare to hope to assist our queer peers for the right to be out and proud globally. The fight is not over; in fact, it's really only just begun.

And so, lesbians, my queer pals and family, it's time to reclaim the L in LGBTQ+ and to go out there and live like you've never lived before. There are only positives that can come from us working on the liberation of our label as the ripple effects reach those around the world who can't speak for themselves. The L comes first for a reason, and as we've heard throughout this book from the likes of Lucy and Stell and Wegan, we've been intrinsic to the freedom of our community thus far. I know that change can be uncomfortable if the word lesbian hasn't held a positive association for you until now, and for some of us, gay, queer or even unicorn, for all I care, might still be where you feel you sit best. However you identify, please know that it's a gift that you're here, and I am so excited that you're on the path to love and acceptance of yourself. How bloody exciting! Navigating the highs and lows of life makes it all the more sweet when you reach a sense of peace, confidence and understanding of your deepest self. But on the journey to getting there, be kind to you, and don't forget to Live, Laugh, Lesbian.

In case you made it this far and still need one last gentle nudge in the direction of self-love...

Stay true to yourself and do whatever the f*ck you want. If you've identified as a lesbian for the last five years and are now finding yourself in a position where you're curious about a man, go explore that! You don't have to confine yourself to one box. Do whatever your heart feels drawn to, love and accept it regardless. That's when you will truly be free.

Emily Gracin

You are loved. You are very much appreciated and loved and you matter and you are enough. That's all you need to know, that you're loved and just never stop being who you are. Because who you are is incredible.

Alissa Butt

Put a little bit more trust in yourself, not in other people. There are going to be people in life who may never fully understand or accept you, but as long as you accept yourself, everything else will follow.

Parisa Tarjomani

In a world that often feels like it's working against you, prioritize yourself above all and nurture the things that bring you joy.

Penelope Gwen

R: I don't care what anyone says, this is who I am and I'm proud of it.

N: We make the world go round, we bring colour to life. Especially in the industries that are here to entertain, there's no world without us in it. It's beautiful that we're all in one community because it highlights our differences and what makes us the same, too.

Rose Frimpong and Nana Duncan

You'll only regret the things that you don't do. If you were to get to eighty years old and were looking back on your life and you hadn't lived it authentically to yourself, would you regret that more than had you come out and lost a few friends? Be brave, be you and remember that you always have family in the queer community.

Jess Gardham and Heather Grogan

Don't compare yourself to other people online. No relationship is perfect; no one is perfect. There's no rush to come out. Be patient, make sure you're surrounded by your friends and your family, and talk to people. And just know that (and this is so cheesy but...) it does actually get better. There's so many queer people out here that are living proof of that.

Cambell Kenneford

You are worthy of both love and self-love, regardless of how you identify, regardless of where you are in your story, and regardless of what others might say. Tune out the noise, and trust that you know yourself better than anyone else. Your love is beautiful in all of its forms. And to the entire LGBTQIA+ community, thank you for being you. Love is love!

Kelsey Pearson and Luke Pearson

Your queerness cannot be put on hold, but you can be patient with it. Take time to be open with your queer identity, because for me, even though I knew it was there, I never deleted it, I never got rid of it. I just knew it wasn't the right time for me. Everybody's got a different time, so be patient with your queerness.

Jade Laurice

Living as your full, authentic self will be one of the most empowering things you do. But it can take time, and it's never too late. Express your sexuality at your own pace, when you feel safe and happy to do so. We all have our own timeframe.

Abi Fellows

Whenever someone makes you feel like you can't be your authentic self just remember this quote: 'Seeing where you don't want to be gives you the drive to strive for better.'

Venus Libido

Don't seek outside validation of your queerness. Haters will always hate. Even our own community can be cruel to one another. Know that your queerness is intrinsic and completely unique and no one can validate that except yourself.

Skylar Mundy

Being part of the LGBTQIA+ community can be the biggest blessing but also finding your way there can be hard. You have one life and you must live it to the best of your ability. Know that you are loved and seen and there is always a space for you. Gravitate to where it feels like home and find your tribe; there is a big community just waiting to love you. Accept your fabulousness, your uniqueness, your similarities, your quirks, your kinks and accept the most amazing part of who you are – YOU!

Lucy London and Stella London

We're proud to live our lives openly as lesbians and as wife and wife. Growing up we both used to hate the word lesbian but now we see it as reclaimed and beautiful. Live your life for you, not others. You deserve to be happy and to live a fulfilled, authentic and loving life.

Whitney Bacon-Evans and Megan Bacon-Evans

My queer sib – I love and accept all of you. For who you are today and for who you will be in the future – as we are ever-changing. A perfectly imperfect human creation, you belong here, you always did. I'm sorry if anyone ever made you feel like you didn't.

Natalie Lee

It's a risk coming out in the first place, so take another risk and go meet some new people who can help you on your journey. Go where you're loved first. Sometimes it's good to branch out in different ways; you don't have to just run to your family first. Go and find your tribe, and we'll help each other figure it out.

Shantania Beckford

Notes

1   https://www.sageusa.org/wp-content/uploads/2018/05/sageusa-the-facts-on-lgbt-aging.pdf
2   https://www.nbcnews.com/feature/nbc-out/nearly-1-5-young-adults-say-they-re-not-straight-n1270003
3   https://www.hrc.org/news/hrc-report-startling-data-reveals-half-of-lgbtq-employees-in-us-remain-clos
4   https://www.stonewall.org.uk/lgbt-britain-work-report
5   https://www.mckinsey.com/featured-insights/diversity-and-inclusion/how-the-lgbtq-plus-community-fares-in-the-workplace
6   https://www.bbc.com/worklife/article/20210526-the-risks-of-coming-out-at-work
7   https://www.mckinsey.com/featured-insights/diversity-and-inclusion/how-the-lgbtq-plus-community-fares-in-the-workplace
8   https://www.researchgate.net/publication/249406253_How_Does_the_Gender_of_Parents_Matter
9   Hetherington, E.M. and Kelly, J. (2003) *For Better or for Worse: Divorce Reconsidered.* New York: W.W. Norton.
10 https://www.bath.ac.uk/announcements/social-media-break-improves-mental-health-new-study/
11 https://www.mentalhealth.org.uk/explore-mental-health/publications/how-look-after-your-mental-health-using-exercise

Acknowledgements

I spent a lot of time on Google when I first had the idea for *Live, Laugh, Lesbian*, researching how to take my idea from thought to thing. Coming up with a plan, a pitch, a way to make this thing happen. The book itself I knew was in me; I'd lived it after all.

The title came to me before the first chapter did and has always been the heart of the book. In a way, I consider it to be my life motto. To live life to the fullest, to laugh and grow through all of my mistakes and to pay homage to the lesbian identity that I feel has given me so much in this life.

After researching heavily, I knew I'd need a chapter, a fantastic pitch to get the ball rolling and finally, a literary agent to take it over the finish line as, let's face it, my forte is more sex toys than book deals. There was a lot to do as a novice writer, and thankfully the universe stepped in to help with a chance online meeting with Abi Fellows (who you'll have heard from in the book) from The Good Literary Agency. If you've read her piece, you'll understand why we hit it off straight away, and her immediate love and passion for the book made me realize for the first time that this might just happen! I signed with her and we waited for pitching season to come in.

My management team at the time saw my pitch, nodded kindly, and then tore into that bad boy like their lives depended on it. And thank god they did, as the first time we pitched out using my basic bitch version, not one publisher came back with an offer. Will, Siang and Carmela worked some fairy godmother-style magic on it and when I saw it, I cried. They had completely captured the essence of the book and presented it in a way that was so sleek and fabulous, I knew there and then that our second pitch round was going to be successful. Without their reworking, I'm not sure I'd be writing these acknowledgements today. I'd also like to mention Craig and Adam here; you're part of this journey, too.

I drank a lot of Champagne that day, and I've been a pushy cow ever since. I may be a writer now but I'm still a Sagittarius with no patience for timeframes, and they've been extremely supportive in letting me plough forward with this book at speed. I'm so grateful that they trusted me, that they championed my title and ultimately my community.

The contributors throughout the book have each been a blessing. I started out by doing Zoom calls, hours and hours of conversations with each of them so kindly sharing their lives with me. All of them have bared their souls to make a home in these pages so that you can find a home in yourself, and I still pinch myself every day that they agreed to be a part of this.

Thank you to every single person I've mentioned, and to those who have made this book possible. Nothing has made me feel more fulfilled in my life than writing this, in the hopes that it helps even just one queer person hug themselves a little tighter when they put it down. Thank you for being a part of something truly magical.

Mamma Bean, Pops, Becky and Fran. Your unending faith in me is priceless, and look. I wrote a book!

Jessica Kingsley
Publishers

JKP is a leading specialist global publisher at the forefront of social change. We aim to promote positive change in society and encourage social justice by making information and knowledge available in an accessible way.

Our specialist areas span autism and neurodiversity, health, social care, mental health, education, disability, gender, sexuality and complementary health and bodywork.

We're committed to publishing books that promote diversity and inclusion, including representation of diverse race and heritage, disability, neurodiversity, gender, sexual orientation, age, socio-economic status, religion and culture.

If you have an idea which you think would fit JKP's publishing, you can tell us about it directly by completing a proposal form at

https://uk.jkp.com/pages/write-for-us